HOW DID THEY DO THAT?

Career Highlights, Triumphs, and Challenges

DEBORAH TOMPKINS JOHNSON

Carpenter's Son Publishing

How Did They Do That? Career Highlights, Triumphs, and Challenges

Published by Carpenter's Son Publishing, Franklin, Tennessee

Published in association with Larry Carpenter of Christian Book Services, LLC
www.christianbookservices.com

Cover and Interior Layout Design by Suzanne Lawing

Editing by Virginia Bowen and Lorraine-Bossé Smith

Printed in the United States of America

978-0-9883043-5-2

Acknowledgements

I thank God for the start and completion of *How Did They Do That?* He allows and provides for every good thing I do.

Also, I appreciate my husband Reuben for his love and patience; Sharon Norris Elliott's *Authorize Me* book writing workshop, a pivotal help in gaining structure for *How Did They Do That?;* Marilyn Underwood, for her kind assistance in helping me secure an appointment with Blair Underwood and for needed additional materials; Eva Teig Hardy for her encouragement at the beginning of this project and for assistance and advice along the journey; Alexandria Mayor William Euille, as well as John Porter and Marilyn Patterson, for their assistance in contacting Coach Herman Boone; Rich Doud with the Arlington Chamber of Commerce for his introduction to Gen. Carl H. McNair, Jr.; Brenda Cornelison for coaching me to completion; and to all my family, friends, my church, and coworkers who supported and encouraged me.

Go Ahead . . .

. . . feel free to write in this book. You might hesitate to write in a book because we do tend to cherish them. However, I urge you to write in *How Did They Do That?* I hope you will not only read it, but actually use it. If you are using an e-reader, you can apply an electronic memo or notes function to record your thoughts, or you can go the "old-fashioned" way and keep some paper handy.

I usually take notes while I read non-fiction, the writing reinforces, and helps me recall and apply, what I have read. I invite you to write in the margins or the comment boxes provided on some of the following pages. This book is for you! Mark it up, and make it yours. You can do it!

I believe you will enjoy learning about the experiences and backgrounds of the people in this book. I have benefitted greatly from each person's stories, anecdotes, knowledge, and encounters. I'm excited to share these twelve personalities with you. As I conducted the interviews, recorded them, and transcribed them, the lessons from the people I profiled continuously poured into me. For many months, I have personally worked to emulate some of the behaviors discussed, implemented advice, and made changes suggested. You are invited to read each profile two, three times, or more, and then reflect on how you can use some of the information to benefit your life or the life of someone you know. Enjoy!

Deborah Tompkins Johnson

Contents

Foreword 9

Introduction 11

The Dancer: Elisabeth Hazel Bell 13

The Coach: Herman Boone 27

The Fashion Stylist: Niki Hall 41

The Teacher: Centenarian Ruth Haymon 53

The Songwriter: Dr. Negleatha Jones Johnson 63

The Diplomat: Kathryn Koob 75

The Soldier: General Carl H. McNair, Jr.. 85

The Minister: Rev. Dr. Johnny Parker 101

The Corporate Executive: Sherman Parker 111

The Entrepreneurs: Jack & Magee Spencer 119

The Actor: Blair Underwood 131

The Politician: L. Douglas Wilder 143

A Note to Parents, Guardians, Relatives, and Friends 153

Resources. 155

Foreword

For the past several years I have followed and, at times, interfaced with the career of a remarkably intelligent and equally talented professional woman, Deborah Tompkins Johnson. When she asked me to write the foreword for her latest book, *How Did They Do That?*, I was honored and intrigued. It gave me an opportunity to learn what compilation of skills twelve successful people of all ages and diverse career choices may have in common. It also allowed me to enjoy the insights of an accomplished author, a successful corporate executive, and an eminently respected citizen.

How Did They Do That? is a refreshingly honest and introspective look at men and women who were able to become somebody even though nobody would have suggested such during their childhoods. None of them came from wealth or enjoyed a favored social standing as a result of another family member's accomplishments. And, none of them could expect to receive a "leg up" in life because of a special connection with someone somewhere—except their relationship with God Almighty. All of these life-shaping characteristics are shared by Deborah Johnson.

There are clear similarities among all those Deborah interviewed. Each person placed a high value on education—in the classroom and on-the-job training. All of them valued the role modeling of their parent(s) and/or grandparents—particularly with an immeasurable commitment to a rigorous work ethic. And all were immensely committed and focused, early in life or throughout their careers, to recognize a challenging opportunity for professional growth and advancement when it was there—sometimes offered, but in most cases created through their own determination.

Some compelling and specific insights to success were given by each. Coach Herman Boone sacrificed his time in constant planning to maximize what young boys would learn from his coaching style. Similarly, General Carl H. McNair, Jr. always took on more responsibility than was expected of him, and applied a life lesson to put family first.

Governor L. Douglas Wilder reminds us to "always keep your word," and when you reach your goals, set new goals and reach again. The Spencers remind us that "planning and preparation" are indispensable in creating your own corporate enterprise.

Weaving through all the chapters are personal reflections of the omnipotent power of God. Actor Blair Underwood tells us we benefit if we "follow God's guidance" and "we are never on our own."

Centenarian Ruth Haymon speaks of the importance of living by biblical principles. She is joined by corporate executive Sherman Parker when he says, "we are not alone" in life. Similarly, Dr. Johnny Parker exhorts his love for the Bible and recommends quiet time to get closer to God and ourselves.

Kathryn Koob knows the value of "a strong religious foundation" when one's life expectancy as a political hostage in Iran is uncertain, for her, 444 days. Less threatened, but every bit as purposeful, the lives of those in the cultural arts, like dancer Elisabeth Bell, fashion stylist Niki Hall, and songwriter Negleatha Johnson remind us to reflect on our faith as we walk through life with family, as well as on the frequently lonely path to success.

There are lessons to be learned in this engaging book. I hope, as a reader, you will recognize that when it comes to determining "how they did that," the examples have been expanded to include an even "baker's dozen," as Deborah Johnson has given something for each of us to contemplate and learn from, just as I have from knowing her and reading her book.

Gary L. Jones, PhD
Chief Executive Officer
Youth for Tomorrow
(A New Life Center, Prince William County, VA)
www.youthfortomorrow.org

Introduction

We all want to achieve, and we all want to overcome our struggles. No matter what we have accomplished, many of us have additional aspirations. No matter our age, we desire to expand our knowledge. Since we can gain so much from other's experiences, I introduce *How Did They Do That?—Career Highlights, Triumphs, and Challenges* so we may study people who have chosen a path and achieved success. *How Did They Do That?* shares the insights of people who have endured a struggle or crisis in life.

The idea we can watch a person do something, or observe what someone has achieved, and easily emulate them seems pervasive. I became compelled to talk to accomplished people from different walks of life to gain some insight into what makes them successful. While we may appreciate they had to work hard to attain their mastery, we truly don't know all that was required to reach their level of success until we have "walked a mile in their shoes."

How Did They Do That? takes us a few steps along that mile by profiling twelve people who have made significant accomplishments, while enduring life's challenges or crises. We'll hear firsthand about their goals, work habits, and the influence of others in their lives. These are their stories as told to me.

THE DANCER

ELISABETH HAZEL BELL

Elisabeth studied dance at the renowned Alvin Ailey American Dance Center and the Dance Theater of Harlem, and was selected as a student to dance with The Ailey Company, as well as Ballet International in Indiana. She went on to dance professionally with the Dayton Ballet, Philadanco, and the European casts of *The Lion King* and *CATS*.

Elisabeth fell in love with dance as a toddler. She decided and committed early in life to pursue the rigor of ballet. Commitment to dance was easy for her, though the mental toughness and body work of a professional dancer proved arduous.

HOW DID SHE DO THAT?

Elisabeth shared with me a family story told to her many times: She and her mother were visiting her mother's sister in Tampa, Florida, and while watching a televised ballroom dancing show, Elisabeth turned to them and said, "I can do that." They challenged Elisabeth to show them. With her ten-year-old cousin as her dance partner, Elisabeth, at the age of three, astonished her mother and aunt with a convincing imitation of the professional dance pair. Soon after the revelation in Tampa, Elisabeth's stated interest in dance led her mother to enroll Elisabeth in ballet classes.

Elisabeth's ability to imitate movement proved beneficial over the years, following requests and artistic demands of choreographers and dance artistic directors as she auditioned and performed. While she received much encouragement from teachers, relatives, and friends, Elisabeth credits her mother as the central supporting figure in her successful dance career.

"I am Elisabeth Bell. I have been a professional dancer for more than twenty years, having danced in America with several companies, including the renowned Alvin Ailey Dance Company. I then ventured over to Europe, where I have had lovely experiences in life and dance, namely in The Lion King *and with* CATS *as a dancer and now in an assistant director's role. Here is more about how I did that . . ."*

The Dancer's Story

The Dance Decision

"I am pretty fortunate. I guess I always knew I was going to be a dancer, as I don't remember an 'ah-hah moment.' I enjoyed taking gymnastics as well. I went back and forth between gymnastics and dance for a while. Then I felt like something happened, and I decided I would stick with dance. After that, I never stopped. I never questioned whether I could make dance a career. Instead, I believed if I continued to study and practice, something positive would happen from my efforts."

Daily Regimen of a Dance Student

"My routine was to come home from school, maybe have an hour or hour and a half before going to ballet class, then come back home, do homework, and dinner, or dinner and homework, and go to bed. I definitely remember attending McDonough School, a private college preparatory school, where things became more difficult because my school days were longer. Of course, the amount of homework increased, too. When I was seven and eight, I might have had ballet twice a week, but when I got older and started at McDonough, they recommended four to five times a week.

"When I was five, I enrolled at the Sudbrook Arts Center for additional dance classes. I probably was ten or eleven when I started working with the first core group of dancers, though they were all older than me. I remember I was one of the tallest, but also the youngest."

Summer Camps

"I had the majority of my dance training at Sudbrook, but some summers I was able to go to dance camp. The Ailey Camp, an outreach program sponsored by the Ailey school in New York, had a camp for inner-city youth. My mom learned about the camp because she worked for the Baltimore City school system, and was able to get me into the camp the summer of eighth grade. She couldn't afford to send me away to dance camps because those were thousands of dollars just for a couple of weeks. She would find local classes to get me supplemental training, at places like the Morton Street Dance Center and Kinetics Dance Theatre.

"At the time, ballet class was everything to me. Missing a day—a week, God forbid a month, of classes—gave me anxiety that I would relapse into a non-trained dancer. I needed to be in class. I remember in high school, my mother wanted me to do an exchange program to France. I was like, 'Well, I am not going to miss my ballet classes!' And that's how I thought.

"I don't think I have the same audacity I did as a teenager. I definitely knew at fifteen what I wanted to achieve. Although I've attained my goal to have a steady career in dance, doubts of my own abilities became more prevalent later in my career than before I became a professional."

Not Just Dance, Ballet

"Definitely, my interest in dance has always been in ballet. Many told me my body type wasn't necessarily going to be the best for ballet, but I never really listened to them because ballet was what I enjoyed doing. In the end, the ballet technique made me an all-around dancer.

"I once had a teacher who compared me to another dancer. She told me, 'Elisabeth, this other dancer is a ballet dancer, but you're a good dancer.' I was taken aback, but I also knew the things I struggled with were true obstacles to being a good ballet dancer. For instance, I didn't have the high instep or the 'good feet' to have the normal aesthetic lines of a ballet dancer. In fact, my journey into pointe shoes was quite an ordeal. Luckily, the one thing physically I had was flexibility in my extensions. I had the gusto and the audacity to push myself in auditions and performances. I found I surprised people. They didn't expect me to do the things I could at certain times. Often my response to discouraging comments was, 'OK, yeah you say that, but I'm

"LUCKILY, THE ONE THING PHYSICALLY I HAD WAS FLEXIBILITY IN MY EXTENSIONS. I HAD THE GUSTO AND THE AUDACITY TO PUSH MYSELF IN AUDITIONS AND PERFORMANCES."

not going to let that deter me.'

"The teacher who did not consider me a ballet dancer might have been the most influential teacher I had. I'll never forget what she said to me when I was fourteen or fifteen. I learned a fine line exists between encouraging young people to realize their dreams, and helping them to be quite realistic.

"Another time, I received a scholarship to the Dance Theatre of Harlem, and my teacher said, 'Actually, I see you more as an Alvin Ailey dancer.' I thought, 'I don't want to be an Ailey dancer! I want to do ballet!' What do you know, two years after, I was at the Ailey School. Funny how things develop, but that's the irony of it all. Two years after I rolled my eyes at the suggestion of modern dance, I ended up at Ailey, which was, of course, quite beneficial."

On to College

"I needed more training, so I decided to study dance in college. My mother allowed me to look at colleges where I could major in dance. I'll never forget visiting a university in New York because it had a reputable dance department. The head of the dance department told me, 'Well, clearly since you're pursuing college—and not already dancing professionally—you're never going to dance in the New York City Ballet or for any major company.' I knew many dancers were affiliated with companies at fourteen or fifteen, but I couldn't imagine going to a school where the department head would tell me what I wouldn't be able to do versus what I could.

"Well, I selected Butler University for its strong ballet emphasis. Everyone in dance had to take ballet five times per week, no matter what year you were. And the other classes—the modern, the jazz, even tap—were also a part of my degree. Other than the dance program, Butler didn't offer me much else. Socially, I had a hard time fitting in, but I stayed at Butler and held onto knowing I was getting a superior dance education. My class started with twenty dancers, and we graduated with thirteen or fourteen. Maybe six or seven of us actually worked as professional dancers. The others had the skills as well, but they found they had other interests."

Indianapolis to Dayton to Philadelphia

"My studies at Butler, and all I had done prior, paid off. I got through auditions and was invited to join Dayton Ballet, where I stayed two years. In my second season with Dayton, I started job hunting and began auditioning with other companies. I did well in the auditions. Not all of them led to a job, but the fact I got through the entire audition and was still competitive was rewarding.

"I actually had to audition twice for Philadanco, the company I later joined. At Philadanco's January audition, I had an 'I am back' feeling. I had been having issues with my turns at work at Dayton, and triple pirouettes were required for one of the ballet auditions. That day, the pirouettes were a breeze for me. I said to myself, 'Elisabeth, you can do this.' Also, I could definitely see the reaction of some of the other dancers who were watching my audition. I'll never forget the reaction of one of the company members: 'Who is this? Girlfriend, you just came out of nowhere. Your legs were up, and you were just twirling!' He was quite a character. His reaction and elation for me gave me such a good feeling.

"Getting the job at Philadanco was very gratifying. Even more amazing was the chance to work with Joan Myers Brown, the founder and director of Philadanco, who is definitely a force to be reckoned with. Philadanco is her baby, and she nurtures her hired dancers because of the personal investment she has in her company. When she hired me, she told me, 'You're too much of a ballet dancer right now, but we can work with you.' My reaction was, 'Finally, someone is calling me a ballet dancer!' Having someone show faith in me gave me the boost I needed at the time. She and the rehearsal director coached me to always go deeper and to tell the story through my body. Because of my experience at Philadanco, I ultimately became an artist, not just a dancer."

Daily Regimen of a Professional Dancer

"I would definitely say after college and once I was in a career as a dancer, I began exploring ways to stay fit and injury free. In Dayton, we were required to have a membership with the local YMCA, the director's motto being how dancers are athletes who needed conditioning as athletes. That's when I started becoming acquainted with Pilates and yoga. I used to think having a flat stomach was equivalent to having a strong core. Pilates quickly corrected my mistaken belief.

"Stretching and other exercises are daily regimens that help dancers achieve their maximum on stage and in the studio. Dance is an art form, but it is also a sport. Dayton Ballet's rigorous six-day-a-week schedule had me literally unable to walk in the mornings. I first had to stretch to get the blood flow going. I would wake up and do ten minutes of crunches, and that, of course, was *after* I was able to crack out my legs so I could walk over to the TV and put in the abs video.

> "I REALIZED WAITING TO BE AT WORK TO START MY PREPARATIONS WASN'T SMART. I NEEDED TO CONSTANTLY WORK ON MY BODY FOR WHAT WAS TO COME . . ."

"At Philadanco, we worked in the evening, so I would take supplemental classes when I could. A ballet studio located in the suburbs had excellent training, and one of the universities also offered free classes for Philadanco dancers. I had my own yoga video I would do at home. I was just trying to prepare my body for the demands of Philadanco and its touring schedule. I realized waiting to be at work to start my preparations wasn't smart. I needed to constantly work on my body for what was to come, and then I would have regular massages to restore and rebalance my body from the strains of it all."

New York Visit Leads Way to Europe

"Down time was rare, but on one of my breaks, I went to New York to see friends I met when I was with Dayton Ballet. They were with the Dayton Contemporary Dance Company and were performing at Brooklyn Academy of Music [BAM]. During my visit, a group of us decided we would go to France the following summer. I was very excited because I had never been to Europe.

"A good friend, Julius Brewster, and I were the two to take the reins to organize everything. Originally, we intended to include six people, which was really perfect because Julius and I had similar expectations on how to best organize the trip. We agreed we would have contracts and deposits, because we knew some might be fickle and pull out. We were looking at lodging in France, and we depended on everyone participating and paying their portion since we all had very modest incomes as dancers. We started with six and we ended up with just the two of us in the end, with the deposits of the others defraying our costs. The two of us ended up going to Paris together and had a fabulous time. We discovered we were great travel buddies and decided the following year to go to Spain together. And because we had such a lovely time with the woman we stayed with the first time we went to Paris, we wound up returning. We felt so liberated in the more relaxed lifestyle in France."

More Paths to Europe

"In February 2006, Philadanco got the opportunity to work at the University of Florida in Tallahassee for two weeks with two internationally known choreographers, one from Japan and the other from Holland. We were able to collaborate and create without the pressures of having to produce a viable piece, a luxury in this day and age. In March, Philadanco toured Germany for a month. The exposure was all I needed to start wanting something different.

"After leaving Philadanco, I planned to begin with a workshop in Amsterdam with the Dutch choreographer I had met in Florida. I had a list of companies I was interested in auditioning for, but I knew the summer months were not normally when auditions were held. I was prepared to bide my time with my 'we shall see' philosophy."

Job Opportunities

"My travels took me to Berlin, where I moved around a bit, staying with different artists I had serendipitously met while I looked for work. Two weeks into taking classes at different studios in the city, someone passed my name to a choreographer who needed to replace a dancer in Cottbus, a former East German city outside of Berlin. The phone call came. After two weeks, I had a job as a 'guest dancer' at a State Theatre. Initially, I was quite stressed getting started with the State Theatre. They knew I was foreign, but they assumed I had been living in Germany and had the proper paperwork for employment. However, I did not. Another dancer who could speak both English and German was summoned to translate and aid me in the process. After a bit of back and forth and cajoling, the approval to work in Germany was stamped in my passport.

"I had a set rehearsal period and specific dates throughout the month to perform. I was quite fortunate to have had steady income, freedom to look for a more permanent job, and time to travel and be spontaneous."

Serendipity in Action

"Once again, my path hadn't been quite as I intended, but rewarding, nonetheless. My first two-and-a-half years in Germany, I was able to have the college-type experience socially I didn't have when I was a college student in The States. In Germany, I met new people and opened myself up more, allowing the wind to blow me in whatever direction, simply because I could.

"If someone said, 'I'm going to XYZ,' I would say, 'OK, I can go.' Time is precious, and to have the luxury to explore without time constraints was simply priceless. The privilege to experience that kind of freedom allowed me to return to my normal self, perfectly content to stay at home.

"I began looking for another job when I learned *The Lion King* in Hamburg was looking to cast dancers. I really had never had any interest in musical theatre, but my thought was, 'If you are invited to the audition, go. You never know . . .' What was intended to be a fallback ended up being my only offer and how I entered the musical theatre world. In my first contract in *The Lion King*, I portrayed the cheetah. In the second season, I became a swing performer, covering all of the dance ensemble roles."

Very Different Dance and Musical Experiences

"Then I auditioned for *CATS*. What a change! While both are musicals,

The Lion King and *CATS* are quite different. In *CATS*, each person is playing a role. Almost every character has individual lines to sing. I have to say, in doing *CATS*, I was able to gain an appreciation of what being a musical performer means. I didn't fully appreciate that before I did this show. What is vocally asked of everyone while still performing as a dancer is truly amazing. *CATS* represents the true definition of the musical genre where every member dances, sings, and acts—all at the same time.

"In *CATS*, you are full-out singing and full-out dancing—at the same time! No one is hired as just a singer, and no one is hired as just a dancer. *Everyone* has to do *everything*. Once I mastered the dual roles, I felt a great accomplishment. I thought, 'OK, this isn't easy, but I can do it.'"

The Next Step is Now

"*CATS* is admittedly a hard and demanding show. I got to a place in my life where I started contemplating my next steps. I just didn't have the physical energy to prepare myself eight times a week in the same manner I had previously done. I had to acknowledge the changes in my stamina.

"The timing worked out perfectly. The director was leaving and needed to be replaced. The producers at *CATS* took a leap of faith with me. Wanting to rebuild the creative team of the show, they offered me the assistant resident director's position. I had worked as a cast representative for two seasons with *CATS*, proving myself to be a communicator. I had a good rapport with both the cast and the management. I had the opportunity to let them see I was pragmatic."

A Move to Artistic Direction

"The producers actually offered me a chance to both move up in the organization, and still perform, but I knew if I were still performing I would have lost my hair just from the stress. I know how I am. I am a very focused individual. If I do something, I want to do it right and give it my undivided attention, hence my over twenty years of dancing.

"I am not focused on performing now. I'm working on the organizational and artistic side. My body is not under the same demands it has been, though I do have a clause in my contract where I will perform in an emergency situation. I think this is a perfect segue for me to experience not being a primary performer.

"As assistant resident director, I have to learn the show in and out—as if I am the resident director. Since the resident director will still be performing, my responsibility is to act as resident director when he is on stage. That entails knowing the show—all the roles of all twenty-three cats on the stage. I must know not only the choreography, but of course, the story behind why everyone is doing what they're doing. I need to understand the music, the lights, what the show is, and maintain the performance standard. I rehearse and prepare understudies as well. Basically, I'm learning the show choreographically, the staging of it, and also learning and memorizing the full text. That's a lot of text, and it's in German. I have to stay diligent."

Moving Forward While Reflecting

"I have to say, I really find myself pulling from my past experiences, both the good and the bad, to find my way in this new role, acknowledging the importance of encouragement, yet honest feedback. I'm picturing myself as a part of a creative team dedicated to making sure the performers in CATS see themselves develop. My role is really about helping everybody reach their maximum potential. Once again, I've been blessed. Things didn't have to work out this way.

"I'm actually OK not dancing full-time. I'm usually quite thoughtful when I make a decision. I have listened to my body and have had inner dialogue with myself to know and feel I have made the right decision. I have also seized a wonderful opportunity. We'll see in six months if I say the same thing! But, for the moment, I feel very blessed, and I'm OK with my decision. I always say, 'We will see.' That's my motto, and I'm open.

> "I HAVE LISTENED TO MY BODY AND HAVE HAD INNER DIALOGUE WITH MYSELF TO KNOW AND FEEL I HAVE MADE THE RIGHT DECISION."

"Thankfully, I reached my dream and goal in life to have a career as a dancer, to actually earn money as a dancer. I'm not a starving artist, which had been one of my mother's fears. Well, that's not the case. I can fly home to Baltimore, or travel on vacation, or just treat myself on occasion. I have truly been blessed. I have nothing to complain about. I've had the ups and downs of life like any other person, but I'm fortunate I have had an education, and I've been able to use my education to do the things I've wanted to do. I try not to take for granted any of the things I've experienced. When I do have moments of uncertainty, I take comfort in the lyrics from a hymn I like, 'Lead me. Guide me along the way. Lord if you lead me, I cannot stray. Lord, let me walk each day with thee. Lead me, oh Lord, lead me.'"

WOW

Words of Wisdom from Elisabeth Bell

Excellence . . . "Whether you're twenty and performing—or you're forty-five and performing—you want to keep growing. You want feedback. You don't always want to be told you're fabulous, because you're usually not. Even people who are good or excellent want to improve themselves. That is usually what makes them excellent. They are never satisfied."

Confidence . . . "Having confidence is half the battle. Sometimes that's more than half the battle because sometimes you must convince someone you know what you are doing, even though you don't. Sometimes that someone is quite often you. Mastering one's own self-doubt, giving yourself the chance to succeed or maybe even to fail, is key to opening up the possibility to excel."

What Can **YOU** Do Now?

"You've read my story and my WOWs—Words of Wisdom—now, what about you?

"Whether you are an adult making life decisions on your own, or a parent considering dance study for your child, you have similar next steps. With regard to picking the best means of training, one just has to look at the quality of dancers the school produces. The visible skill of a dancer is the best advertisement for a school. Good instructors and good schools are bound to have students who have made a viable career in the profession.

"To excel in dance today, one must master everything. You can't snub your nose at ballet, jazz, or modern dance. In this *So You Think You Can Dance* age, dancers have to be prepared to do all forms of dance. Sometimes one has to fake it to make it. The more one can offer, the better. The dance profession is too demanding physically and mentally without joy and passion to carry you through. Perseverance, diligence, and fastidiousness in one's training are also critical to set you apart from the rest. Start as early as you can and don't stop."

Dear Reader,

Here is space for your notes, thoughts, or next steps:

The Coach
Herman Boone

Herman Boone, once a poor youngster, has become a highly sought speaker, following his celebrated success as a football coach who understood the requirements to bring about change. As head coach of Virginia's 1971 Titans football team, Coach Boone and his players won all their games, and the athletic excitement helped to bring unity among the players and to the City of Alexandria.

How Did He Do That?

Herman Boone faced many experiences—as a child and as an adult—that challenged his human and civil rights. Choosing not to back down, but rather face his detractors, Boone became an advocate for social justice and the betterment of the African-American race, and of all young people.

Coach Boone peppers his speeches, as well as his one-on-one conversations, with tough-love expectations and the need for no-nonsense behavior. Like many of us, Herman Boone repeats the phrase, "Our children will have to replace us as leaders." Therefore, he pursued teaching to influence youth and to help mold boys and girls into responsible men and women who could contribute positively to our society. Beyond teaching, he knew coaching could not only produce winning teams, but if done right, could lead team members to find commonalities in order to develop relationships and depend on each other, on the field and off.

Coach Boone says he took a while to find his way, but once he did, he became a determined person, and now claims the song, "I Did It My Way," as his motto.

"I am Herman Boone. I fought through challenges and overcame obstacles until I could live my life my way. I travel throughout the US and abroad to tell young people they can win, grow, and succeed. I became a winning football coach and committed teacher who helped to grow children into responsible adults. Here's more on how I did that . . ."

The Coach's Story

Talking the Talk—The Beginning of Change

"When I took the Alexandria job, I knew I had to become a leader of change. And this is why I struggled so much to get people who didn't like each other to talk to each other—just talk. Talk about what? I don't know, just talk. If you can talk to people, you no doubt will probably find something about them you can relate to, something about them that transcends narrow-minded thinking. If you can talk to a person, then just maybe you can learn to accept their soul rather than reject them because they are black or white. Where did I get this from? I don't know, but conversation has proven a true remedy in difficult relationships."

Athletics and Activism

"I didn't set out to be a Martin Luther King or a Moses. I think I fall more into the Ferdinand Day of Alexandria [Virginia] class. Day, who was on the school board when I came to Alexandria, is a man of explicit intelligence who has a tremendous sense of humor and a personality that soothes the savage beast, just by being around him, seeing and feeling what he believes in, and how he plans to make a difference. I learned from Ferdinand Day how to control my anger and turn it into something positive, because I had the opportunity. I had people around me looking for my leadership, and other people wanting me to fail. If you are positive about your life, believe in yourself, and have faith, failure is not an option.

"In 1956, I had bouts with my faith when my mother, father, and sister died one behind the other all in the same year. Death tends to test your belief and your foundation.

"My faith has always been the foundation of my life. For me, it's a very private thing, but I will tell you I do have my moments with the person responsible for the whole universe.

"My faith has never been far from my profession, or my life as a husband or as a father. Although, some people say I lack good faith for as much as I used to curse, but that's neither here nor there as far as I am concerned. It's what you believe in. To believe is to have faith."

Golf Caddie to Advocate

"A lot happened in my life, making me the person needed in the situation in Alexandria. One particular incident occurred when I was a teen and probably shaped me and how I respond to people, situations, and mistreatment: I remember, in 1954, I was desperately in love with a little girl named Ethel Mae. Ethel Mae was a church-going girl. I didn't have the right shoes to go to church to be with Ethel Mae. I had a pair of brogans. Back then, brogans were shoes symbolizing the poor. This friend of mine said I could go to the golf course and caddie for two days, and I could make enough money to get some penny loafers. They were very popular, and if you had a pair of penny loafers, man, you were somebody.

"I went out to the golf course to caddie for the first time. The caddie master came to the door with this bag of clubs. Many of the caddies were veterans. Veterans had come back from World War II and didn't have any jobs, so they would go out and caddie. Well, the caddie master would favor the veterans because many of them had families.

"Anyway, the veterans split. All of the veterans ran away from the bag. They took off and left me standing alone. The caddie master said to me, 'Come on, Ike (my nickname). Here's a bag for you.' I was glad to get the bag. I didn't know whose it was, but it meant two dollars for me. I looked up and here comes this little white man, shuffling, who couldn't walk more than three steps a minute, coming down to the tee. I realized why the veterans didn't want the bag—he was so slow and rarely, if ever, played more than two holes. On the second hole, he called me over and said, 'Come here, boy.' He pulled an awful bloody, cotton handkerchief from his pants and handed it to me to take to the woods. I said, 'I don't want to touch it.' He proceeded to curse me out, took a club out of the bag, and swung it at me. To protect myself I backed up and ran through the woods until I got home.

"The next morning, I was awakened by my mother beating me with my father's shaving strap. I was wondering, 'Why are you beating up on me?' Well, a policeman had come to my house that morning and told my mother

her son had sassed one of the golfers. Now 'sassed,' in the black community or the black vernacular or language, meant you disrespected somebody. The policeman said the golfer was my mother's landlord, and if my mother wanted to stay in his house, she'd better take care of her boy, and man did she. I was barely fourteen, and being beaten almost to death so we could stay in that house remained with me a long time.

"The underlying thought behind the whole thing is: I could have turned violent or negative, but I chose to use my unfair beating and policeman's interruption at my home as a commitment to speak up and speak out. From that day on, I dedicated my life to never being placed in a position where people would make me guilty of a crime based on the color of my skin. I became an advocate for civil rights."

> "I COULD HAVE TURNED VIOLENT OR NEGATIVE, BUT I CHOSE TO USE MY UNFAIR BEATING AND POLICEMAN'S INTERRUPTION AT MY HOME AS A COMMITMENT TO SPEAK UP AND SPEAK OUT."

Teaching and Coaching—A Good Pair

"Schools, like any other place, are not immune to injustice. I decided teaching would be a good way for me to make a difference. Also, I admired my high school coach, Dave Ackerson, so much I just wanted to be another Dave Ackerson. Consequently, I pursued coaching as well as teaching.

"I learned teaching is about changing attitudes. Yes, we change attitudes for the short time on the football field for practice, but we interact with the players during the regular school day and become a little bit more involved in their lives other than just football.

"Being around the kids and letting them see you beyond the football field as a human being who cares, who intervenes on some parts of the school system which are unjust to them, is important. Students face tough situations, and they need to know they can come to you when the girlfriend is pregnant, when they want to quit school, when they want to get married at sixteen, or when they need someone when the guy they saw in the house this morning was the tenth guy coming out of his mother's bed, and he wants to shoot him. More than anything else, they need someone when their mother is on crack, and they want to throw her out the top window.

"This makes coaching and teaching synonymous with caring. You can't fake caring. Kids know when you are genuinely involved in their lives, and that's what teaching is all about."

School of Hard Knocks

"My first job—teaching and coaching—was in Blackstone, Virginia. I stayed in Virginia three years but wanted to go back to North Carolina. In 1961, I did, but met controversy when I returned to my home state.

"I often say I went to Williamston, North Carolina, as a colored boy. By the time I took my knocks, and knocks, and knocks, I left a proud black man. After we started practicing football, I went down to the drug store, established an account, and bought tape and medicine—things for bruises and stuff. I made the mistake of sitting down in the booth to wait for the pharmacist. The sign said, Whites Only. I noticed the pharmacist wouldn't wait on me even when he was free. When he finally got to me, he said he wouldn't wait on me as long as I was sitting in the white booth. I said, 'Well, what color is it? I didn't see a white booth.' I think the booths were blue or pink. I hadn't even been there three weeks when that happened."

Hard Knocks Too Close to Home

"Later, I had a chance to meet with Dr. King [civil rights leader Martin Luther King, Jr.] in Edenton, North Carolina, and it got publicized. The school board didn't like it, and neither did the Klan. I know they didn't, because they tried to bomb my house! They made a mistake and bombed my next door neighbor's house, though. He was an invalid and never got involved in anything. Afterwards, even the principal asked me to leave for the sake of my family, so we wouldn't get killed.

"But we stayed, and in between all of this came ninety-nine football games with only nine losses, an extraordinary record under extreme circumstances and adversity. In spite of these incidents, through everything, my teams were able to win five championships.

"In 1969, after winning the fifth state championship, I was in the bank cashing my paycheck and so was the superintendent, who said to me, 'Congratulations Coach Boone, you brought pride to the community.' I remember verbatim what he said. 'North Carolina just passed a $100 million bond issue. Martin County is going to get $1.3 million from that bond. We are now the first test case for Richard Nixon on integration. So we are thinking we are going to have to spend this $1.3 million in building a central high school to integrate the schools. With you as assistant coach, we can't help but win, can we?' I said, 'What did you say?' He said it again, 'With you as assistant coach, we can't help but win, can we?' Now, let me describe this young coach they wanted me to assist.

"IN SPITE OF THESE INCIDENTS, THROUGH EVERYTHING, MY TEAMS WERE ABLE TO WIN FIVE CHAMPIONSHIPS."

"He was a twenty-one or twenty-two-year-old white guy. His first year out of East Carolina, he lost his first nine games. He won his tenth game. He was 1-9. One of his players got thrown out of the tenth game for an infraction of some kind. The coach changed the boy's jersey and sent him back in. The state took that game away from him. He was 0-10, and I'm going to have to assist someone at 0-10 when I am 99-9? 'I don't care if he's pink,' I told the superintendent. 'Not by the hair of your chinny, chin, chin. I am thirty-five years old, and I've lost only nine games in my entire life. I've given this county ten years, and the best you can offer me is to assist a twenty-two-year-old kid who cannot carry my boots?' Denzel quoted me verbatim in the movie [Oscar-winning actor, Denzel Washington, portrayed Coach Boone in the movie, *Remember the Titans*]. Needless to say, I was not very happy with leaders in Williamston and their plan."

Finally, a Breakthrough

"A change was coming, and it began at a national college football annual clinic held at the Willard Hotel in Washington, DC. Blacks couldn't eat at the Willard Hotel, though. We could attend the clinic, but we had to eat at Howard University, until I and three other coaches met Bear Bryant, Frank Broyes of Arkansas, and the Texas coach, Darryl Royal. They asked us, 'Are you boys having a good time at the conference?' I said, 'No.' 'What?' Bryant asked. 'No. We're not.' 'Why not?' Bryant persisted. I said, 'We're not having a good time because we can't eat here like the rest of the coaches. We have to drive all the way up Georgia Avenue to eat at Howard University.' Bear Bryant of Alabama had no blacks on his team; neither did Darryl Royal or Frank Broyle. Bear Bryant went to the manager of the Willard Hotel. I don't know what he said to the hotel manager, but he got permission for us to eat at the Willard.

"We probably integrated the Willard Hotel—me, Paul Hines, Cecil Short from Charles County, and the coach from Fairmont Heights High School in Maryland.

"I TOLD THEM, 'YOU SAID YOU WERE LOOKING FOR A BLACK COACH. I AM NOT A BLACK COACH. I AM A COACH WHO *HAPPENS* TO BE BLACK AND PROUD OF IT.'"

"Another thing happened at the football conference that year. T.C. Williams High School football staff, all white, along with the athletic director, came to my room and said, 'We are looking for a black coach named Herman Boone.' Nobody said anything. 'Do you all know a black coach named Herman Boone?' Still nobody said anything. 'Well, we heard he's been fired in North Carolina, and we need a black coach; we heard he is dynamite.' I'm sitting listening, and finally they left not knowing the person they were looking for was in the room.

"The next day, the T.C. Williams staff came back and said, 'We found out you were in the room, and we want to talk with you.' I told them, 'You said you were looking for a black coach. I am not a black coach. I am a coach who *happens* to be black and proud of it.' I almost lost that job, too.

"Well anyway, they gave me a contract for $14,785. I thought I had died and gone to heaven! I was only making $2,700 in Williamston. My principal was making $5,000 a year. The superintendent was making $10,000 a year. I decided to take the job, and that's how I got to Alexandria."

Big Challenge, Little Loyalty

"The next year, Alexandria consolidated the three high schools for total integration. Little did I know or care to know, they named me head coach of the newly consolidated high school over a legendary white coach with a steadfast following and a reputation second to none, not only in Alexandria, but in the entire state of Virginia. The only reason I became head coach over [William] Bill Yoast was because they already had nineteen white head coaches in the city and no blacks. Had I been in a sport other than football, Yoast would have been head football coach, but because I was in football, and they had no other black coaches, they named me over Yoast.

"Quite frankly, I was scared to death. They didn't even ask if I wanted the job. They assigned me the job, and it came out in the newspaper in July, before school started in the fall.

"I went to the superintendent and told him, 'I do not want the job. I did not ask for this job, and it is totally unfair to Coach Yoast.' The superintendent pulled out my contract and said, 'Did you sign this contract?' You'd be stupid to say no, so yes, my signature was on it. 'Did you read this contract?' You'd be even more stupid to say no.

"Well, the last paragraph in the contract says, 'If you accept a teaching position in Alexandria and an extracurricular activity, and if you resign from one during the school year, you resign from both.' I had just left North Carolina, wife pregnant with the second child. Where could I go? I had to drop my pride and accept the job.

"Did I think I could do the job? Yes, with reservations: I could not select my assistant coaches. All of my assistant coaches were once Coach Yoast's assistant coaches. Where was their loyalty?

"I got the superintendent to give me the right to add one coach. I went to Charles County and got my friend, Paul Hines, who had been with me throughout the turbulent years. He was the only black coach up here I knew who was available.

"The school board didn't want to cause any more hardship in the transition than they necessarily had to. All of the coaches had been abused—they said—so they were not going to allow me to choose all of my assistants. This meant I had little or no loyalty with my coaching staff."

The Secret: Practice Schedules

"I won games anyway because I fought hard. I planned hard, and I demanded perfection through my practice schedules. I couldn't go up to the new students face-to-face and tell them, 'You will do this, and you will do that,' and expect to get good results. However, when I handed them their practice schedule which told them they could get a drink from 2:00 to 2:01, or they could only use the bathroom from 3:00 to 3:05, what choice did they have? They had to follow my practice schedule. I exerted my discipline and my philosophy through my practice schedule.

"I told the assistant coaches, 'I will call all the plays from the one yard line into the end zone, and all the plays from the one yard line coming out to the twenty yard line on this team, because this is where coaches get fired. I've never seen an assistant coach get fired for losing a game. Therefore, I will make all the decisions in the red zone.'

"I think I knew I had to win and win big because remember, the football program is the first program of the school year. It was the first program through this experimental desegregation program, controversial as it was. The success of the football team generally would be passed on as success for this total desegregation program. The failure of the football team would be looked upon as a failure of desegregation in Alexandria.

"The way I saw it, the entire consolidation program was viewed as successful if the first athletic program of the season was successful. Had the football team been unsuccessful—it is written, and I can show it to you—then the consolidation program would have been a failure. They didn't expect me to win, but I worked hard. I stayed up at night while they were asleep. I broke down game film while they were out drinking beer. This proves what I often say, 'Success comes from hard work.'

"Maybe I did have a purpose for being here. Maybe the purpose of my mother's landlord swinging the golf club at me because I wouldn't take his bloody handkerchief was what I needed to be different. You know, when you wake up every day, you do what you think is right. Maybe that's making a difference. Wake up with an intention of making a difference. Do something that's meaningful.

"I could have gone either way; I was sure angry enough. I could have been a lot of things—bad things, negative things our children are struggling with today. At the time, people didn't think blacks were worth anything, so why be anything? This is where I heard no one should ever be allowed to make you what they want you to be so they can laugh at you for what you are.

"I don't know why I chose the other way, which was considered the right way. I don't know, and I probably won't ever know. Maybe I was destined. Maybe God had a plan for me. I don't know. I never really gave it much thought.

"We've talked about me a lot, but not so much about the Titans, not really. Let me tell you something about the Titans, and then let me tell you something about the movie, *Remember the Titans*.

"Yes, the Titans won football games. That was fantastic, but those young athletes were also molded into dynamic human beings and became fathers throughout their chosen cities in America today, which, to me, was even more important than winning football games, although we had to win. At the time in Alexandria, we had to win. You couldn't fool around and not win in Alexandria and expect to keep your job.

"I'll just say this: The movie *Remember the Titans* is not about football. The movie *Remember the Titans* is about some incredible young men who, by learning to talk to one another when it wasn't popular in Virginia, learned the importance of celebrating their differences and not allowing their differences to become a problem to be solved."

Words of Wisdom from Herman Boone

Athletics . . . "All great football coaches spend at least two hours developing their practice schedule, because you must guide people—as a leader—from the moment you blow the whistle to start practice, to the moment you blow it to end practice. You must be totally organized. I decided to keep my practice schedule tight. Therefore, we had no room for confusion, which meant no time for dissension."

Life . . . "Hard work is the first thing. My philosophy on success is it's only a word that comes in front of hard work. Hard work causes you to be successful, not your looks. I even told Denzel this. Success is what you put in your craft; it's what you put in your profession.

"If you are at your desk an hour or two hours before those who expect to learn something from you, you can be prepared to give them something they never heard. Successful people are not nine to five people."

Leadership . . . "If you can take one thing away, leadership is about people willing and able to make changes. Leadership is about change."

What Can **YOU** Do Now?

"You've read my story and my WOWs—Words of Wisdom—now, what about you?

"I give these next few words to young men: Whether you want to be a coach and teacher, a corporate executive, or laborer, pull up those pants when you go for the interview. Put on a belt; groom your hair; shine your shoes. Then, you can walk into an office for a job interview or walk into a bank and seek a loan.

"I know the styles of today, but you don't have to make the rumpled kind of outfit part of your life in general. You can't go in the bank to borrow money or expect to get hired unless you have a professional look. Sometimes you have to pull up your pants and put on a shirt and tie."

Dear Reader,

Here is space for your notes, thoughts, or next steps:

The Fashion Stylist
Niki Hall

Based in the fashion industry's hub of New York City, Niki Hall can now claim success as a fashion stylist. Niki's versatile work consists of creating outfits for entertainers' performances at various venues, dreaming up characters for film, flaunting fashion trends for magazines, and other times giving full-service wardrobe assistance to professional athletes and national television personalities.

How Did She Do That?

Like many in the artist, creative, or entertainment fields, Niki struggled for about four years at the onset of her career in New York, not knowing when the next job in fashion would materialize. While seeking a breakthrough in the fashion industry, Niki took jobs at clothing boutiques, restaurants, or bars.

Her initial years in fashion proved grueling, and Niki experienced a short relapse in 2006. Disheartened and tired of the hustle of New York City, she returned to her mother's home in Virginia, succumbing to the repeated forays into fashion styling that proved too limiting financially.

Thankfully, Niki's mother and sisters stepped in. She appreciates them for having had faith in her talent and skills, and for encouraging her with a "You can do it" mantra. Her family's intercession reminded Niki she never felt motivated or particularly connected to Virginia. As they continued to reassure her during her three-week stay at home, Niki said their support gave her the fuel she needed to give New York another go.

A supportive environment, and the necessary education and skills combined to develop Niki's flourishing fashion career.

"I am Niki Hall. I came to New York City with a dream to excel in a career in fashion. Humbly, I can tell you, I strive to continue to learn more, but I have built an impressive clientele and have begun to make a very good living creating styles for national broadcasters, famous entertainers, and more recently, professional athletes. Here's some of my story on how I did that . . ."

The Fashion Stylist's Story

Things and People Fall into Place

"When offered opportunities to follow my heart's desire, I took them. I had gone to New York City during a summer break from Howard University in Washington DC. When I got to New York, I felt like I was in the right place at the right time, and I just had to see where it was going to lead me. If fashion design in New York City didn't turn out as I hoped, then I could always come back to the DC area and return to Howard. However, I felt I owed myself a chance, because a career in fashion was a quiet dream inside.

"I had to find ways to get noticed. I went to as many fashion and entertainment events I could, which led me to meet a lot of great people, many of whom I am still friendly with today. Essentially, the summer just before September 11th in New York, my best friend Ayana Van Putten and I fell into the field of styling. She and I used to get dressed up in these crazy outfits. We'd think of a theme from a movie or a concept a bit over the top and get decked out as a means to get into events. We just wanted to go wherever the party was and get into fashion shows as a way to get noticed. One night, we met this event photographer, Johnny Nunez. He asked us if we were stylists. Even though we had such a strong interest in fashion, we realized we didn't fully even understand what styling entailed. He said, 'You guys should; you'd be great in the fashion industry.' Throughout the summer, he started introducing us to people as stylists and opened up a lot of conversations, which eventually led to work.

"We happened to meet Patricia Field, who was styling *Sex and the City* at the time. We kept seeing her out at different events. Then maybe about a month later, we saw her again out at this party. Ayana dared me to ask her to have lunch with us so we could pick her brain about her journey as a stylist, and have her mentor us.

"This story might sound far-fetched, but it's true: We were at this hot club of the day called Bungalow 8 and happened to be sitting at a table with Jay-Z [Grammy and Tony-winning musical artist and entrepreneur], and Nelly Furtado [Grammy award-winning singer, songwriter, and actress].

Ayana's friend managed Nelly Furtado, and that's how we ended up at the table with her and Jay-Z. We saw Patricia Field at the venue, and I asked if she would have lunch with us. She said, 'Yeah, I've seen you around. I'll have lunch with you girls, only if you introduce me to Jay-Z.' I took her over to the table and introduced her to Jay-Z.

"She kept her word, too, and the next week, we had brunch with her. We met with her maybe twice and also chatted with her on the phone several times. She gave us encouragement we needed to take the plunge . . . encouragement, but kind of at a distance. She told us she liked our style, thought we had what it takes to be stylists, we should just do it, and we didn't need an agent or a portfolio; we just had to do it. She said we had to determine what we wanted to do and how much our time was worth and just do it!

"I think, from that moment, what she said about stepping out there gave me a little bit more confidence. We started to believe in ourselves and networked with people accordingly.

"Later, we got acquainted with these guys who were starting an indie street-culture magazine in New York called *Frank151 Book*, and were looking to incorporate fashion. We got thrown into it. We learned how to come up with story concepts, hire photographers, hair and make-up artists, cast models, pull clothes, and secure a location. We truly had a trial-by-fire experience.

"We got paid very little. The magazine owners took care of some of the expenses, but it was very minimal. However, the three years we contributed to the magazine opened up so many doors for us. We worked with different people in a variety of settings, which is one of the main things I like most about my job. You're forced to develop a sense of community quickly. A project might last a day or for several weeks, usually a very brief amount of time. We easily cultivated close bonds with other artists on a creative level. We were impacting each other and working toward something together. We developed a rolodex of people who we continuously recommend for work. In fact, two of the big contracts I have now—one with a major broadcasting network, and the other with the NBA—were obtained via referrals from colleagues."

Major Contracts, Famous Clients

"I have a roster of a few TV broadcasters for whom I purchase clothing for their daily on-air appearances. I work with them to develop a concise look from head to toe, and shop for them on a weekly basis. Then, I meet with them in their homes for fitting. At most, I only need two meetings with someone face-to-face to fully grasp his or her style and/or physical attributes. Overall, my philosophy is people have to be comfortable with what they are wearing, so I try not to impose my own personal tastes upon them. I make sure I understand the kind of look or vibe they want and decide how to take it from there: shop, borrow, or have items custom made.

"My work with the NBA entails more designing and wardrobe management than styling. My team and I work in collaboration with the NBA's creative director and producers to conceptualize the designs for the cheerleaders and the dancers to wear throughout the events, as well as the celebrity performers for the all-star games' half-time show. I have seamstresses and tailors who work with me and do the actual sewing, which takes almost two months. We always run into unexpected needs at the last minute, but overall, each year presents a great but rewarding challenge to outdo the previous year.

> "MY PHILOSOPHY IS PEOPLE HAVE TO BE COMFORTABLE WITH WHAT THEY ARE WEARING, SO I TRY NOT TO IMPOSE MY OWN PERSONAL TASTES UPON THEM. I MAKE SURE I UNDERSTAND THE KIND OF LOOK OR VIBE THEY WANT AND DECIDE HOW TO TAKE IT FROM THERE."

"For instance, three years ago one of the celebrities performing during the three-day all-star event wanted rhinestone stripes on his tracksuit for his appearance. He wanted a very specific type of topaz-colored Swarovski crystal rhinestones, no less. The challenge was wandering through Los Angeles—a city I was not familiar with—going on a scavenger hunt of sorts to figure out where to obtain the rhinestones. Social networking proved to be a great resource in tracking down places. I tweeted about my search and got tremendously helpful responses about places that would have the rhinestones. I took nearly three whole days to find all of the 2,000 rhinestones required. One of the tailors working on it sewed each of them on by hand in virtually only a day.

"A lot of times with big productions where I'm dressing multiple people, I need to hire people to work with me to achieve the goal. I'm giving them cash, or I'm giving them credit cards, trusting them. The majority of the time, I only contract people who are highly recommended or who have worked with other people I know. Very rarely do I hire someone I don't know or someone I know doesn't know. That's pretty much how I get all of my jobs as well—through word-of-mouth or recommendation. We help each other out.

> "I LEARNED HOW TO DO THAT—TO MAKE THE IMPOSSIBLE POSSIBLE. I DON'T GIVE UP UNTIL I FIND A WAY TO SOLVE THE PROBLEM."

"The other aspect of my job I like is the problem-solving factor. Each project presents its own constraints, be it time, money, or both. Producing something right for all parties involved, and simultaneously making that happen within a limited time frame, can be extremely nerve racking.

"I learned how to do that—to make the impossible possible. I don't give up until I find a way to solve the problem."

Accountability and Credibility

"I have been tried by fire, but I now understand the importance of exhibiting a level of professionalism at all times. The fine details can make the most impact.

"Though I might have 300 pieces of clothing, I still know where everything is and where it came from. I've always kept an eye on each piece of clothing and importantly, every dollar. Because I am using other people's money to shop, I invoke a great sense of accountability and responsibility to deliver the best possible results. If at the end of the day something goes missing and it can't be returned or I don't have a receipt to show for it, then it comes out of my pocket.

"You might conclude correctly I spend a large chunk of my time doing accounting work. I didn't think it would be that way, but the more my business grows, the more time I need to take care of the financial details. I don't mind doing the accounting, as I have always liked crunching numbers. I like to understand and know how money is moving in and out. The most time-consuming aspect is keeping track of and reconciling all of the receipts, making sure the right amount is spent and not overspent, basically staying within the allotted budget. I'm shopping for items and then maybe something doesn't work. I may have to take it back, return it, or exchange it, and then prices might be different. The process of tracking everything gets kind of meticulous."

Not Always a Good Fit

"I don't like to have too much down time between jobs. I enjoy staying busy, but I have to sometimes decline a job. Whenever I say 'no,' it's usually because of the time constraints, whether I think it's worth the amount of time I would have to put in, the amount of stress, or if enough time is allowed to do what a potential client needs. For instance, recently someone emailed me in the morning to see if I could style two people that day for a reality TV show, which is not impossible. I didn't want to stress myself out that much, though. Usually, I need at least one full day to do that type of work, and that's pushing it.

"Another time, I had the opportunity to work with a really famous singer. I went to meet her and spent the day observing to see if I wanted to accept a contract with her. I decided not to work with her because I didn't like the way she treated her staff. When I was in high school, I really admired her and I thought, 'Oh I would love to work with her,' but we clashed, and it just wasn't worth the amount of stress to me."

Starting Early, Starting Right

"My work often has some type of stress, though, but I am happy with my career. A career in fashion is something I wanted for a long time. Since I could remember, I've been into clothes and fascinated by texture and color. In high school, my fashion merchandising instructor, Deanna McCoy, took the class on a trip to New York to catch a glimpse of what this fashion world was about. We toured the Fashion Institute of Technology and had lunch at the chic, model-owned Fashion Café, which Naomi Campbell, Claudia Schiffer, and Cindy Crawford had opened in their heyday. That visit to New York solidified my desire to work in fashion.

"My fashion classes in high school in Fairfax County were very instrumental in exposing me to various creative outlets. I also took a jewelry design course. One of my teachers, Joan Morgan, recommended me to a friend of hers who was a silversmith in need of an apprentice. I worked with Yvonne Arritt for about three years, assisting her in the production of hand-made silverware, bowls, sculpture, and jewelry she sold at juried craft shows like the Smithsonian Craft Show and the American Craft Council shows.

"I traveled with her to the shows, which helped me understand the possibilities of being an artist on one's own terms. Not only was she creative, but she was a smart business woman. A lot of the stuff I made for her was actually commissioned by and sold at the Smithsonian gift shop in Washington, DC, and I witnessed her struggles and her worrying about selling her art. She was a major influence on my life in terms of believing I could actually make a living doing something creative that I truly loved. Yvonne taught me how to understand and appreciate quality design. Just seeing this woman operate her business on her own made an impression on me. She did the accounting and the creative. I think she showed me my dream was possible."

Family Influence and Encouragement

"Even before the high school field trip and apprenticeship, I was about five when I began to tell my mom, 'When I grow up, I'm moving to New York to work in fashion.' She encouraged me and told me I could be and do whatever I wanted. She always supported my creative endeavors.

"Starting around the age of twelve, I became fascinated with fashion magazines. I'd always beg my mom to buy me one at the grocery store, primarily *Vogue, Mademoiselle,* or *Jane Magazine.* I'd just flip through the pages, devouring as much as I could on a visual level. I didn't really read the articles; I was just drawn to the images and the clothing.

"My Aunt Linda used to make most of her and my cousin's clothing. My older cousin, Tammy, used to do these illustrations for me when I was around five. I think this was the initial spark within me."

Speaking, Believing, Giving

"I'm not going to say my career has been a bed of roses. I'm not perfect. I've definitely been burned and tried. For a while I got caught up in the glamour of fashion and living the New York lifestyle. Also, when I was younger, I was prone to be pessimistic, discouraged, and negative thinking.

"My mom had an antidote. She suggested I start speaking daily affirmations—positive statements I wanted to happen in my life, such as, 'I am creative. Jobs flow to me effortlessly and easily.' Some of them I pulled from a book; some of them I drew from Joyce Meyer, a charismatic speaker I like; others, I wrote on my own. I had them taped to my wall, and I would say them out loud when I woke up in the morning every day for about two years. I really saw a shift in my mental outlook on life. Sometimes when I need to pep myself up, I still say them. It really does help. I believe our words have power, and our mind is powerful. If we convince ourselves we can't do something, then we won't be able to achieve that endeavor. However, if we believe we can, then we can! Getting to a goal might take longer than we thought, and we'll always have obstacles or trials.

"I definitely think my faith has played a large part in me believing in myself, in being exposed to people who were willing to give me a chance, and to doors being opened.

"I also believe in giving back to others financially—by tithing. It doesn't have to necessarily be to a church or religious affiliation. The law of giving and receiving has shaped my life tremendously. Once I started really giving consistently, I found my career taking off in a different way. I still believe giving back to some kind of cause you believe in is very important. Whether you give to a church, charity, or a cause, your efforts to help others will aid you in the end.

"I think I'm finally at a point where I've seen financial success, but I want to continue to grow and challenge myself. My work makes me feel alive. It's stressful, but not enough stress to say, 'Ah, I don't want to do this anymore.' In the midst of some fashion or business challenges, I have definitely said this to myself, but at the end of the day, just seeing something I've helped create or helping someone look their best, gives me great fulfillment."

Words of Wisdom from Niki Hall

Listening . . . "I had to learn fashion styling is not only about what I want specifically, or what I think looks good. That's where the editorial comes in—I'm allowed to express myself on those types of jobs, but I have to be respectful of other people's ideas and opinions."

Serving . . . "I have found working as a team member helps me and is usually necessary. Some stylists I've seen on TV might not be willing to do the menial tasks required, even if their assistants are sweating, and time is running out. I don't mind stepping in, steaming, or doing something. I like to work as a team and want to make the people who work with me feel like we're working together, and not like they're working for me, because a lot of times, I simply can't physically do all that needs to be done by myself. Fashion can be a small industry. If you behave poorly, selfishly, or in a superior way, word will get around."

What Can You Do Now?

"You've read my story and my WOWs—Words of Wisdom—now, what about you?

"I will expound on the advice given to me: You don't need to necessarily have what you think you need in order to do something you want to do. You don't necessarily need an agent. You don't necessarily need a hefty portfolio. You do need to meet people and find your way around to people in the fashion business, or people you might see as future clients.

"The fashion industry is both competitive and subjective, so loving yourself and believing in yourself are very important. Also, love others in terms of the way you treat people, whether they're your family or your work associate.

"To some degree, be realistic in your expectations, but if you're passionate about something, don't take 'no' for an answer. You must have stamina and staying power. The pace in fashion is incredible, with a lot of time constraints; being professional and learning how to manage people's personalities is also critical. Don't allow them to rock you off your composure.

"Be reliable in terms of managing clients' money wisely and accurately. Be professional, show up on time, and work diligently to do the job you're asked to do. Be sure to show you are passionate about the job so people know you're serious. When you don't have a work ethic, people will see it. You have to be willing to turn over every leaf to find the perfect 'whatever' the client wants or needs. You have to come to the table with something relevant to show them or even present ideas they weren't possibly thinking about. You must 'deliver' on time.

"Write down what you want and expect for your life and speak it out loud.

"Finally, if you want to see some styles of one person in the fashion industry and the styles I created for several of my clients, visit my website at www.nikihall.com, and also follow me on Twitter at https://twitter.com/thisis_NIKI."

Dear Reader,

Here is space for your notes, thoughts, or next steps:

The Teacher
Centenarian Ruth Haymon

Mrs. Ruth M. Haymon, a centenarian born November 6, 1910, taught school during the depression era. Although professional careers were scarce to non-existent for black women in the 1930s, Ruth Haymon earned not only a bachelor's degree, but also a master's degree, which supported her professional career in teaching.

How Did She Do That?

Mrs. Haymon says her challenging and rigorous education from the Northern Presbyterian Church, a mission field for educating young southern blacks, along with other experiences, were key.

Coming from a family line of doctors, teachers, merchants, and a tailor, Mrs. Haymon knew she wanted to attend college and originally desired a degree in business. However, those colleges were too far away, too expensive, or excluded blacks. She attended what was called a "normal" school and began her full-time career in teaching.

"I am Ruth Haymon and am more than 100 years old, and thankful to be in good health and to be living in my own home with family. In spite of limited opportunities for African-Americans in the 1930s, I received a great elementary and high school education. Despite the many years required, I went on to obtain my undergraduate and graduate degrees. Even before finishing high school, I became a teacher. Here's my story on how I did that . . ."

The Teacher's Story

Northern Presbyterian Mission Comes South

"I didn't know education would be a part of my life for so long, but as a young girl, I loved to read, and I loved learning. Fortunately, we had a very good private school right across the street from our house I was able to attend while I lived in Cotton Plant, Arkansas. How could a black girl go to a private school in the 1920s? Well, the Northern Presbyterian Church had these mission schools all over the south. I attended two different missionary schools for all of my elementary and high school education. From first to eighth grades, I attended the Presbyterian's Cotton Plant Academy located in my neighborhood.

"I feel I had good training, and I owe a lot to my Presbyterian-based education. I didn't have to endure some of the sub-standard conditions most people went through, because the Presbyterians could teach what and how they wanted because they were privately funded.

> "THE CAMPUS ARRANGEMENT GAVE US MANY CHANCES TO TALK AND SOCIALIZE, WHICH I ENJOYED. I LIKED THE EXPERIENCE OF MINGLING WITH PEOPLE OF ALL DIFFERENT TYPES."

"I remained with the Presbyterian schools, but in the ninth and tenth grades, I transferred to their boarding school for girls in Mississippi called Mary Holmes Seminary. Going away to boarding school really excited me. Teachers and students lived in the upper areas, and the classrooms, chapel, and dining area were on the first floors. The campus arrangement gave us many chances to talk and socialize, which I enjoyed. I liked the experience of mingling with people of all different types.

"For the eleventh and twelfth grades, I came back home and finished my high school years at Cotton Plant Academy. While I attended the academy, I actually taught school where my mother worked. Back then, you could take a test to become a teacher. Anyone who passed would qualify to officially start teaching. I passed, obtained my teacher's certificate, and substitute taught during the summer."

Student or Teacher

"Right after I graduated from Cotton Plant Academy, I got a job with them teaching the fourth grade class. I had problems with a lot of parents because they said I wasn't old enough to know how to teach. They didn't want me punishing their children, and neither did the principal. He wanted me to bring my students to him when they needed disciplining. I told him, 'Well, you don't want me as a teacher then. If I am supposed to be a teacher, then I have to be the one to do whatever is needed. If I can't discipline my own students, then where will my respect be?' He was very strict, and he treated many of the teachers as if they were still his students. Originally when he asked me about teaching at his school, I said, 'No I don't want to teach for you.' He asked me why, and I told him, 'If I am going to teach, I want to be treated as a teacher, not as one of your students.' I suppose I had a lot of nerve. He thought my mother told me to say that, but she didn't even know he had asked me to teach."

Depression Era Teacher and Daughter

"After teaching for my former school, I moved on to study in college while I worked at other schools in Arkansas. My mother helped pay for college, even though getting steady paychecks was a challenge for teachers during the Great Depression. What they were often given in lieu of their salary was a type of promissory note, and merchants would allow limited other types of merchandise per note. To get *real* money, the teachers organized literary programs at school on the weekends. They would work with students on their singing, drama, or poetry to help them put on a play or sometimes a musical. Admission was about five cents, and after the programs, teachers held socials and sold ice cream, cookies, or cupcakes (all homemade) for additional income. Nobody had a lot of money, so they could only charge sometimes a nickel, dime, or quarter each. That money helped the teachers take care of their families, which is how my mother helped me with college."

A Lifetime for College

"I started college at Pine Bluff AM&N [Agriculture, Mechanical, and Normal School] during the depression. At times, I didn't have enough money to buy a postage stamp. One time, my mother had sent me seven dollars to buy food. I got the letter, but I did not get the money because someone had taken it. I did not have three pennies to buy a stamp to let her know I got the letter, but not the money. I don't know how long, maybe a week, I didn't have anything to eat; I got so hungry!

"When I did have a little money, I would buy a big apple. I'd eat half an apple at noon and the other half when I would come home after classes. The apple would be all I had because it was all I could afford.

"Pine Bluff AM&N had a dormitory, but I couldn't afford to stay on the campus. I had an uncle who taught away from home, and he stayed where he taught. Nobody was at his house in Pine Bluff, so he let me stay there, rent free. However, I had to walk five miles across town to get to and from school. You have probably heard many others say the same thing: Yes, I walked so much I wore holes in my shoes.

"The house had a wood stove used for cooking and heat. My uncle paid the light bill, but sometimes I went without heat in the house. When it would rain, I would be soaking wet by the time I got to the house. I'd come in and hang my clothes up to dry, then get in the bed, cover up, and put a light up under the cover, which is where I would prepare my lesson for the next day.

"I had been away at school for only five months when my mother became ill, and I had to return home and I didn't get to finish the year out. I eventually completed my degree requirements by working in the winter and going to school in the summer. Finishing college and getting my master's felt like a lifetime—more than twenty years to get both degrees."

Team Teaching with My Husband

"After getting married, my husband and I both taught at Stamps High School in Lafayette County, Arkansas. The school district hired me for home economics, and my husband for agriculture and mechanics. Stamps High School had agriculture and home economics in the same building. The boys were put in agriculture and mechanics classes—or 'shop' as they called it—and the girls were placed in home economics. My husband and I decided to periodically exchange students so they could learn both sets of skills. The girls had a chance to learn things like how to change faucets, to fix leaks, and to do some light electrical work. My husband taught them how to use a hammer, a yardstick to measure for carpentry, and how to properly use a saw. When the boys came to my class, I taught them how to cook simple meals, sewing, and basic mending. They learned to repair their own clothes—hemming, replacing buttons, and 'turning' worn or torn collars. Those were really interesting years for me.

"Many years later, I stopped at a restaurant to eat. When I went in, I noticed one of my former students was the owner and cook. He said, 'I learned to cook from you. I couldn't find anybody else to be my chef. I finally asked myself why was I getting someone else to be my chef when I can do it myself?' So, he just started cooking and became his own chef. He said, 'What you taught was enough for me.'"

Important Basics

"After two years, I went to work at a school in a rural community in Arkansas where they had only three teachers for first through eighth grades. I had to teach the regular courses: language arts, math, science, social studies, and health. After my first year of teaching, the board permitted additional grades to be added, until classes went to the twelfth grade. At different times I taught from fifth to the twelfth grade. I didn't teach home economics as I did at Stamps, but in the health classes, I tried to teach basic life skills along with the regular class work. I would teach personal hygiene, table manners, and etiquette most of the students had not been taught. My life skill instruction advanced according to what the students were experiencing in their lives."

Healthy Relationships

"For eleventh and twelfth grades, I taught Introduction to Marriage. I advised them sex was for marriage, educated them on preparing for children, and shared what they should instill in their children in order for them to be the kind of person they should be. I went on the religious side because I felt that was necessary. I taught boys how to treat their wives with respect, respect for one another, and when they had children, what their responsibility would be.

"I told them about diseases and how to keep themselves healthy. I discussed with the girls the benefit of not having sex before marriage. I also encouraged the boys and the girls to make goals about the kind of person they wanted to marry and to stick to those goals. I'd say, 'Don't just pick up anybody who comes along.' I wanted each person to be able to make his or her own choice about what they wanted in the other person. 'Remember, you're going to be together a long time; therefore, you need to marry somebody whom you think you can be compatible with,' I would say to them. As I have already stated, I added a lot of biblical principles in my classes. We only had one church in the community, and everyone went to this church. Everyone had about the same upbringing, so the parents were not against me teaching those things. In fact, they were glad because they said they didn't know how to teach their children about health, sex, and parenting.

"I ALSO ENCOURAGED THE BOYS AND THE GIRLS TO MAKE GOALS ABOUT THE KIND OF PERSON THEY WANTED TO MARRY AND TO STICK TO THOSE GOALS. I'D SAY, 'DON'T JUST PICK UP ANYBODY WHO COMES ALONG.'"

"Years later, I had a man approach me whom I didn't know. 'I want to thank you,' he said. 'You have given me the best wife I could ever have. You taught her so many things, making her absolutely a good wife.' I felt that was an accomplishment. Then I had a student who married and resided in Chicago. She and her husband worked for a doctor, and occupied the living quarters above the garage. Her husband took care of the yard and things like that. She helped inside the house. She told me when she got pregnant, the doctor told her not to worry. He would see she had her baby. As she was developing, he would tell her different things, and she would say, 'I already knew that.' The doctor would tell her what she needed to buy, but she had already gotten them. He said to her, 'Well, your mother taught you well.' 'My teacher taught me, not my mother,' she told him. She said she didn't keep notes on everything, but she had a whole notebook on carrying a baby. I educated the boys about pregnancy, as well. A lot of the children didn't know the different parts of their bodies, how to name them, or how to pronounce them. Sometimes they would get bits of information from one another. I taught them the correct names for the different parts of their bodies. 'You've heard the common language, but I want you to hear the correct language,' I told them. I enjoyed teaching them about life, and they seemed to need it.

"Helping so many students was really gratifying, but I did retire from teaching when I reached eligibility at the age of sixty-two. I tell you, life has been even better since then! Not to say my life has been easy and pleasurable all the time, but I have no complaints. I feel very blessed to have come this far."

WOW

Words of Wisdom from Mrs. Ruth Haymon

Listening . . . "Now that I look back, I feel the direction of my life was not me. I feel God directed me. I feel good about the fact I did try to follow and not rebel. Although I didn't want to do a lot of things, I didn't refuse to do them. I was submissive to wherever He led. Knowing I wouldn't have done these things and allowed God to lead me is a good feeling.

"I have tried to be very careful about not making plans without asking the Lord. I do believe fervently in the Lord, and I try to do what He says and not rely on my human nature."

Daily Devotions . . . "As stated previously, I was reared with a religious foundation. I still rely on the Bible. I like to do my Bible study and read books based on the Bible. Every morning, I use my computer to access my daily Bible devotions. Then when I get ready to go to bed, I read something biblical so that will be the last thing I have at night. This routine gives me guidance through the day and good sleep at night."

God and Family . . . "Next to time with God, the most important thing to me is my children. I love to have them visit me or I visit them. They have their own interests and their children, grandchildren, and great grandchildren, but I think my family wants to be around me, too. I am thankful. Maybe people will think I am bragging, but that's not the way I feel in my heart. I just feel I've been blessed."

What Can YOU Do Now?

"You've read my story and my WOWs—Words of Wisdom—now, what about you?

"As I approached and passed 100 years of age, people would ask me how I managed to live so long, stay pretty healthy, and how can they do the same.

"Well, who am I to say? God has everything to do with how long a person lives. The important question is 'Whatever my age, am I living the way God wants me to live?' 'Am I doing what God wants me to do?' I ask myself, 'Why am I still here? What is God's purpose and have I carried it out?'

"If you want to teach, be sure you are dedicated to teaching, training, and improving the lives of the children you teach. You are dealing with lives and not objects. May your goal not be money only, but your interest be in lives."

Dear Reader,

Here is space for your notes, thoughts, or next steps:

THE SONGWRITER
DR. NEGLEATHA JONES JOHNSON

Now a recording artist, songwriter, and minister, Negleatha Johnson, fondly called "Dr. J" by her friends, had attained success in post-secondary education as a well-compensated administrator and faculty member in higher education. She gave up lovely campus surroundings, great pay, and benefits for unpredictable streams of income coming from a full-time music ministry of songwriting, CD releases, live performances, speaking engagements, and foreign mission trips.

HOW DID SHE DO THAT?

An early start with piano lessons and songwriting seemed to be key to Negleatha's musical calling. Negleatha began playing piano at six or seven years old, and the songwriting soon followed. Negleatha wrote her first song—about life in a castle—when her fifth-grade class finished its study of the Middle Ages. Negleatha sang the song with a classmate for a play at Northwest Elementary School in Kinston, North Carolina. At that debut, she fell in love with putting musical concepts together in a way people enjoyed.

"I am Negleatha Johnson. I never really saw myself in music or ministry early on, but from the beginning, I liked writing music and sharing my songs. Now I write, and then speak and sing messages of hope, healing, and restoration for audiences and congregations, not only in the US, but also abroad where I have led two mission trips to Slovakia, three to various cities in Italy, and to Toronto, Canada. Here's more of my story about how I do that . . ."

The Songwriter's Story

Starting Young

"Even before I became aware, I think my music has always been about God, and God in our lives. At ten years old, I became excited about trying to learn more about God. I was just kind of a unique little kid, very aware of God and always wanting to do what was right. I had a strong sense of what was right and wrong. When I look back, I remember feeling God was always with me in a special way. I enjoyed being a teenager and had the typical challenges, but God kept me from a whole lot of madness, Lord knows He did. Through everything, I played piano for church, gave piano lessons, and pretty much did something musical all the time."

Inspired Music

"I started my education at Our Lady of Atonement, a Catholic school in Kinston, North Carolina, where I loved the music and still remember many songs the nuns taught us. The environment and songs were very inspirational and stayed with me. That type of music became a part of me and who I was becoming.

"My mother had my sisters and me in church all the time, I mean ALL the time. She always prayed for us. She was then, and is still, a person of faith. She is inspirational to me, still striving to be the person God wants her to be. She has been a very good example for me.

"Besides my mom and her prayers, another inspiration was my high school choral music teacher, who had an impact on me and how I do what I do today. Mrs. Wynona Rhem, choir director at Kinston High School, was the aunt of an acquaintance at the time, Jimmy Johnson.

"Mrs. Rhem has passed now, but she made an impression on me. She had a way of pushing a group of us high school students and motivating us to experience music in a new way. We would sing songs in Latin and perform a variety of pop and classical tunes. Those songs in other languages and varied genres transported us beyond our world in Kinston, North Carolina. She showed us that something much bigger than our little world existed. I think of her as a person of excellence. She pushed us in the way she pushed herself. When the time came for us to sing in concert, we had to order these wonderful dresses, and the guys wore tuxedos. Her presentation was good. She was very careful not only about what we sang, but *how* we presented ourselves as well. I often

> "THOSE SONGS IN OTHER LANGUAGES AND VARIED GENRES TRANSPORTED US BEYOND OUR WORLD IN KINSTON, NORTH CAROLINA."

reflect on her style when I have to go out in front of an audience or crowd: 'Well, God, am I looking the way you would have me look? Have I prepared accordingly?' Some of her detail for attire, staging, and let's not forget timeliness, definitely apply to the manner I perform today."

A Journey with Two Loves

"Another influence in my life was Mrs. Rhem's nephew, the Jimmy Johnson I mentioned earlier. Jimmy and I reconnected during our college years and later married. Many years into our marriage of now thirty-plus years, Jimmy and I founded and operate Life Waters Ministries. Jimmy handles event arrangements, concert promotion, accounting, and all of the ministry administration pieces. The journey of my songwriting, ministering, and CD releases has taken many unexpected turns.

"When we married, I had planned for a career in music therapy, and Jimmy was active-duty military. Off we went to Missouri, where Jimmy was stationed near a little town of about 1,500 people. I had hoped to teach choral music in the high school, but the school system had just hired the ONE choral music teacher they needed. I had to regroup.

"As much as I appreciate the military and what spouses can contribute to the active-duty soldier, I had to have my own career because I was not one to sit idle. Jimmy was cool with it, so it wasn't a big issue.

"When I was unable to find a job, I prayed and felt led to go back to school for my master's degree in personnel administration at the University of Central Missouri. I saw myself moving away from any career field in music. Three years after completing my degree program, our daughter Zenita was born. Shortly after, we moved to Nebraska when she was only three months old. My first 'real' job in higher education was at the University of Nebraska, where Zenita was able to attend the on-site daycare. It was an exciting time. Over the next several years, the three of us relocated to several different duty stations for Jimmy and more university jobs for me in New Mexico, Nebraska, Kansas, and eventually Virginia. I absolutely loved all my jobs and earned my PhD along the way. God worked everything out for us, and I can't even thank Him enough for all He did for us. I didn't have to pay a dime for my education or for child care. He blessed us every step, at every location.

"But in 1995, the next love of my life, God, who is really my first love, stepped in majorly. In spite of my wonderful job, great office with a lake view, and talented staff, I started feeling restless. I know now God created uneasiness within me about what I was doing. Nothing was wrong with a career in higher education, no doubt about that, but God wanted me to do something different. I didn't know what God had planned, but I knew He was moving me away from teaching, administrative, and policy responsibilities in the higher education field. After many conversations with Jimmy and a whole bunch of praying, I resigned my job. My departure was tearful. Walking away would have been easier if I had problems on the job. Resigning after so many years of work and preparation was a much greater sacrifice, because my academic career was going so well. However, I had to be obedient to what I was hearing. God spoke and said, 'I need you to get back to the order I ordained.' I'm like, 'What?!'

"Then God just started to knit all of the pieces of my life together. We realized we were supposed to embark on a journey in music ministry.

> "THEN GOD JUST STARTED TO KNIT ALL OF THE PIECES OF MY LIFE TOGETHER. WE REALIZED WE WERE SUPPOSED TO EMBARK ON A JOURNEY IN MUSIC MINISTRY."

"I said earlier I considered a career in music therapy. I still accomplished that goal but in a different capacity. In a way, music therapy is what I do. In my opinion, God took my initial dream and put His spin on it, because being in the ministry of music is very therapeutic. It is as if He said, 'OK, we're going to do music therapy in a different way.'

"Here we were—Jimmy, Zenita, and I—traveling in the US and abroad as Life Waters Ministries. I know we're talking about *my* songwriting, but I tell you, I just follow God along His path. I am His pen; God is actually the writer. As for performances, I get very nervous. I have to pray hard before singing every song, whether it's a full concert or one song on a program. I am OK with the anxiety because every time I get behind a microphone, it is all God. He shields me from the fear. Most people think singing comes naturally for me, but it doesn't. The songwriting and singing come after many hours on the piano, with even more hours on my knees praying and staying still long enough to hear God so I can obey."

Pouring Out Our Lives

"A year after leaving my full-time job, we released the CD and song titled *A Life Poured Out*, which I believe will forever be the song we stand on. It is what Life Waters Ministries is really all about, underscoring all we do. No matter how many CDs we do, nothing will ever surpass *A Life Poured Out*, because of all it represents in summing up our commitment to give all and to do all for Christ.

"When I get confused or have those 'this work is too hard' moments, I recommit to pouring myself into the work of songwriting, singing, and ministering. I might not understand why God gives me some words to say or sing or why He gives me a task to do, but it is not for me to question why. He has done so much for me. He has shown Himself to me in my Bible reading and prayer, enabling me to pour myself into Him and into the tasks He gives me, for no other reason than God said to. My commitment to listen intently and be obedient to what He says profoundly affects my music, my messages, and me."

Writing a Song

"I love to write music—arrange music and create lyrics—probably even more than singing sometimes. I would say the work of songwriting is different for everyone. Even each song is different for me, and the process is not necessarily always the same. I don't sit at the piano and say, 'Oh, I think I'm going to write a song today.' As I have tried to say, what I do is let God inspire me so I know the music is from Him, not that I think anything is wrong with sitting down with a songwriting plan. Many composers can do that.

"I've always been inspired by God with music. Usually a piece of a verse or two, or part of a chorus, will come to me. It can come at any time, but new music comes to me most often when I'm praying—all the time when I'm in a peaceful place. Whenever I've had chaos and confusion, I have not written a word, like when my mind has been all in a tizzy. My music is always birthed out of a peaceful place. Even when I produce a song about a hardship, the lyrics and melody don't seem to materialize until I am at a place of peace about what happened."

"I DON'T SIT AT THE PIANO AND SAY, 'OH, I THINK I'M GOING TO WRITE A SONG TODAY.' AS I HAVE TRIED TO SAY, WHAT I DO IS LET GOD INSPIRE ME SO I KNOW THE MUSIC IS FROM HIM."

I Rise Early

"My day starts out with a plan. When I wake up, I have personal devotional time and quiet time with God. At some point during the day or week, my husband Jimmy and I look at the events and engagements we have for the day or for the week, start to prepare for those, and connect with people who work with our ministry to see what needs to be done for that event. We consistently pray for whatever events are coming up.

"Whenever we have an engagement, I don't participate and then go home, never to return or be back in touch. I like to stay in contact with people we have worked with. I want us to build relationships with the people who have invited us—that's really important to me. If they need prayer, want to go to lunch, or talk over some challenges, the door is wide open. Cultivating these relationships doesn't take much time, and I think this is probably one of those things I'm most proud of, because it speaks to the sincerity of our work. We're not trying to just go in, come out, see you later, or not. We care about building God's kingdom, the people who are in His kingdom, and connecting with them.

"In terms of the remainder of the day, our ministry also includes checking on family members, making sure everybody's good . . . fixing some dinner, doing housework, and trying to go to bed at a reasonable time.

"Closing out the day as planned is sometimes difficult because when I am praying and trying to sign off for the day, God may give me a new song. I have to decide whether I think I will remember it when I wake up, which usually does not happen, or whether I should finish praying and go to the piano right then in an attempt to get enough of the melody and lyrics to a point wherein I can work on it the next day.

"Our schedule doesn't abide by the normal clock because God can intervene anytime He wants to. The days go into night, and night into day. I have to remind myself the day belongs to God, and He can have me use it in whatever way He wants."

Writing Time

"I do set aside time to write and get to the piano. Unfortunately, that doesn't always happen. Sometimes, weeks have passed where I have not been able to get to the piano in the way I want because I've been redirected by God. Other times, I have allowed other things to redirect me. I get it wrong sometimes when I believe God has pulled me to one place, but later find out that was not the case. I'll hear God saying, 'No, that was not Me. You did a good thing, but I did not direct you. I really wanted you to spend your time over on this side versus over there.' Therefore, constantly being before God is critical for me."

Alone With God, All by Myself

"Definitely, we believe we are directed to pour ourselves into each event. When we have a particularly major event—not to say every ministry engagement is not important, but when I say major, I mean that Jimmy and I are producing a concert where we are responsible for contracting all the people, ordering the lights, arranging the sound equipment—I've learned after completing that type of outreach, I need to go away for a couple of days to regroup. I'm tired; I'm weary. I'm also excited knowing God brought us through, and we got the victory because God told us to do it. Human fatigue does set in, though. When I try to continue to move in ministry off those fumes, things will not be good.

"I think—as people in ministry who sing and speak—we need to be realistic and not think we have a magic wand we can wave and 'boom,' life will be perfect, even though we are committed and working very hard. Because of the nature of this work called ministry and the awesomeness of God who has called us, we sometimes tend to expect everything to line up really perfectly for us, and it doesn't all the time.

"The beauty of God is He will never give up on us, so we can't give up on Him! Even if we want to resign, He will never quit on us. He constantly presents me with another way of saying 'yes' to Him and another way of encouraging me during difficult times.

"The challenge comes when I want to say, 'This is just too hard.' I really want to go back and do something that feels a little bit more secure. The world tells me I should do certain things or have or be a certain way. The difficulty is saying, 'Hey God, I'm going to stick with You even though others say I should be doing something else.'"

WOW

Words of Wisdom from Dr. Negleatha Jones Johnson

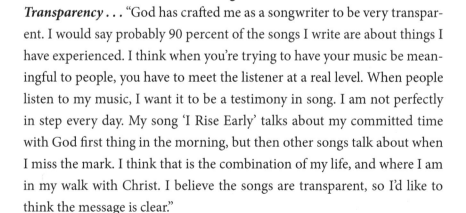

Transparency . . . "God has crafted me as a songwriter to be very transparent. I would say probably 90 percent of the songs I write are about things I have experienced. I think when you're trying to have your music be meaningful to people, you have to meet the listener at a real level. When people listen to my music, I want it to be a testimony in song. I am not perfectly in step every day. My song 'I Rise Early' talks about my committed time with God first thing in the morning, but then other songs talk about when I miss the mark. I think that is the combination of my life, and where I am in my walk with Christ. I believe the songs are transparent, so I'd like to think the message is clear."

His Design . . . "Another thought that comes to my mind, too, is the way God moves us forward is not by the book, but it's by design. In life, that means we look at people who are successful, and we want to imitate them. We want to pattern our success after other vocalists, to see what they did and then imitate it. God says, 'No, it is not by the book, but it is by *My* design—design meaning how I have equipped *you*. I have given you a tailor-made destiny, a tailor-made vision, and a tailor-made anointing along with what I've called you to do. Don't look at what other people are doing. You can be inspired by others, but your path and encounters in life will not be the same as someone else.' That's the difference between inspiration and imitation.

"I think a lot of people become dismayed because accomplishment or success happened quickly for this person, but it didn't work that way for them. I found sometimes, especially when things are difficult and taking more time than I thought they would, my mind begins to look at what God has done for others and I start to compare. I will find myself asking, 'How did she get to do that? She just started yesterday!' God says, 'No, that is not the path I designed for you.'

"As we look at what success is, we have to know God's formula is unique to what He's called us to do, how He has made us, and the things He has caused us to do well. All of those things fit in to *our* design. We can be *inspired* by others, but what ultimately happens is by *His* design."

What Can YOU Do Now?

"I have told you about the path designed for me, now what about you?

"For songwriting, knowing how to play an instrument is a tremendous help. For me, the piano is critical in the process of songwriting. It helps me to hear the harmonies I'm considering for backup vocals and also connects with the tones in my head to bring the sounds to life. No matter how you approach songwriting or the type of music you write—Christian, hip-hop, jazz, blues, whatever—I believe we all need to seek God first. Ask Him about the design He has for your life and your music. Meanwhile, you can prepare yourself.

"Like any discipline, musicians need to continue to hone their skill. Taking a class in basic music theory to understand how sounds go together, what a scale is, and what key signatures are is important. You don't necessarily have to have an advanced degree in music, but at least take a basic theory class or two to understand how best to combine the tones.

"If you are not only going to write songs, but also sing, you need to know how best to tell someone what key you're singing in. If you're getting someone to accompany you and they ask, 'What key is the song in?' and you're saying, 'Well, I really don't know,' that's not good. You need to at least be able to say, 'My song is in the key of F, and we're going to modulate [change keys]. We're going from F to F sharp,' or whatever. Not for the sake of just looking like you know what you're talking about, but because you need to know what you're talking about. Preparation honors God. We perfect our skills in other areas, so we need to do no less with our music as well.

"From a spiritual perspective, take time to understand and examine your relationship with Christ. God's Word is what will sustain you during the challenges, which are inherent in His calling. Make time to read your Bible.

"If you'd like to know more about our ministry activities, appearances, mission trips, CD releases, and other ministry products, visit us at www. lwministriesonline.org."

Dear Reader,
Here is space for your notes, thoughts, or next steps:

THE DIPLOMAT

KATHRYN KOOB

A retired college professor, Kathryn Koob earlier served as a US Foreign Services officer in several embassies throughout the world. While a foreign affairs officer for the US Department of State, Kathryn Koob was taken captive in November of 1979 in Iran. Koob and fifty-one other Americans were held for 444 days when Iranian militants seized the US embassy in Tehran. Koob experienced encouragement and found peace in the midst of the crisis.

HOW DID SHE DO THAT?

Kate, as she likes to be called, credits her upbringing with a strong religious foundation as helping her to endure the thirty-seven months as a hostage, often separated from her State Department colleagues also captured. Kate says she had to lean on her faith for inner strength. She recited Bible verses she knew, and sang songs out loud and in her heart to survive those days in Iran.

"I am Kate Koob. I loved my employment with the State Department, as each assignment abroad held meaningful experiences. The most challenging, of course, was surviving more than a year in captivity in Tehran, Iran. Yet, I emerged with my physical health reasonably intact and with a renewed commitment to study more about the faith that brought me through the hostage ordeal. Here's more of my story about how I did that . . ."

The Diplomat's Story

International Interests

"I have been interested in the world since I was a little girl. I've always enjoyed learning about other lands, other people, and other cultures. I have always been fascinated by history and what makes the world go around, largely due to the number of and varied books my mother had me read.

"Foreign Service was a perfect fit for me, though I had not thought about it and didn't realize I really could do Foreign Service. It was outside of my realm of knowledge until I was in graduate school. I was working on a master's degree at the University of Denver. I was considering law school when I met a woman who said, 'Well have you ever thought about the Foreign Service? The Service has a whole lot of drama, and I think you'd make a good diplomat.'

"I started exploring the idea and discovered a wonderful world of educational and cultural exchanges, which fit right in with my background in terms of literature, reading, and history."

The Right Education at the Right Time

"I was very fortunate my professors at Wartburg College in Iowa and at the University of Denver encouraged us to explore in our fields and to explore outside narrow definitions. Before I took the oral exam for the Foreign Service, I was told 'The best thing you can do is to read as widely as possible, because they're looking for generalists. We can train you in specific knowledge, but we can't train you to have curiosity. We can't train you to think creatively. The diverse skills you learn are really critical.'"

"I WAS VERY FORTUNATE MY PROFESSORS AT WARTBURG COLLEGE IN IOWA AND AT THE UNIVERSITY OF DENVER ENCOURAGED US TO EXPLORE IN OUR FIELDS AND TO EXPLORE OUTSIDE NARROW DEFINITIONS."

Entering the Foreign Service

"I went into the Foreign Service exam totally blind. The woman who encouraged me to find out about the Foreign Service said, 'Promise me you'll write the State Department and find out what you need to do to become a Foreign Service officer.' I sent off my little letter, 'Dear State Department . . .' They wrote back and said, 'The first step is to go to Des Moines and take the test, and here's your entrance card. It starts at eight o'clock on the first Saturday in December.'

"The exam took eight hours. It was the most wide-ranging exam I had ever taken, and I had taken several for my various post-graduate programs. I started taking this exam and thought, 'Wow, this is pretty comprehensive.' At break time, I heard people talking about how many times they had taken the exam and this sort of stuff. Well, I was not used to failing exams. I thought, 'What have I gotten myself into?' The exam had graphs the likes of which I'd never seen before, let alone did I have any idea of how to interpret the diagrams in the economics section. Fortunately, I didn't want to be an economic officer.

"I did pass the exam because I read so very quickly the day of the exam and had read so widely all of my life. I could answer questions about opera, the comic strips, contemporary literature, or history, again just from my wide-ranging background of reading."

The Official Start

"I started with Foreign Service the same way everyone does, in what is called the '100 course, an Introduction to the Foreign Service.' We would come in with a class of recruits and were taught sort of the basic skills of how the State Department functions. We learned how to write reports in the proper State Department format. They told us what our colleagues do, and what an embassy does. We took various courses once assigned to an area. Then we were sent off and had one year as a junior officer-trainee, where we rotated through an overseas embassy doing a variety of things for a lot of different people. After completing our training year, we would be sent off on an initial assignment."

From Favorite to Most Challenging

"I had valuable experiences at each of my posts. My mother would tease me and said she would always wait for her three-week letter: 'Dear Mom: You won't believe it. This is the most fascinating place! The people are so interesting, and we have so much to do and learn here.' I would have to say Vienna was one of my favorite countries; I loved Vienna and Austria the first time I was in Europe. When I got to return some twenty years later to work at the embassy, it was absolutely wonderful. I worked with artists and musicians through an exchange program. In some respects, my assignment in Austria was rather like a dream world with a rich cultural heritage. To be a part of the culture and to watch people celebrate music and the other arts was pretty amazing.

"Every assignment had something of great interest. My first was Abidjan on the Ivory Coast. I had assignments in Australia and Germany, and my assignment in Iran is now certainly historic."

Iranian Student Rebellion

"Sometimes God puts something into your life and says you have to deal with this. I had to deal with being held hostage—being isolated for many days at a time—for more than a year in a hostile foreign country. You must understand, with those who practice traditional Islam—the way I would characterize the college students who kidnapped us—I had no reason to fear sexual violence from the men or women who captured us. Fear for my life . . . yes. Fear of the unknown . . . absolutely.

"Times were unstable. The periods of isolation were dreadful, and not knowing the condition or fate of my colleagues was awful. I was always thinking about how I could communicate with other hostages. At the same time, I had to keep my composure and presence of mind. This all required inner strength. For me, my strength came from God. Many instances I believe God provided directly for my encouragement.

"I HAD TO KEEP MY COMPOSURE AND PRESENCE OF MIND. THIS ALL REQUIRED INNER STRENGTH. FOR ME, MY STRENGTH CAME FROM GOD."

"On the second day of incarceration, I was put into a room by myself. I was lying on the bed sleeping with my face toward the wall, and I felt someone sit down on the bed. I sort of turned over expecting to see one of the young women guards. As I looked around, I realized no one was there. At the same time, I had been sent a message or angel reminding me I was not alone. The verses I remembered from Confirmation were about the comforter from the Book of John, when Jesus said, 'I will send you a comforter.' That was the term I chose to use, 'The Comforter,' and I knew I was not alone. Angels were with me, and so was God."

Desire for Communion

"I had another experience in March that led me to believe I would survive my captivity. For some reason, a movement and agitation among the students arose, and we had hints we might be released. I thought, 'Oh good, maybe we'll be home by the first Sunday in March, and I'll be able to go to communion at my home church.' I was very much desiring Holy Communion. Well later, I clearly knew I would not get home in time for the first Sunday communion at my church. I thought maybe a priest would come visit, and give us an opportunity to worship, because we had visits at Christmas and one other time. I was alone at this point since Ann [Elizabeth Ann Swift, the only other woman held captive the 444 days during the Iran crisis] had not yet become my roommate. Sunday morning I woke up, and I just somehow knew not only would I not be home for communion, but no priest would be bringing me the traditional communion with bread and wine. During my personal Sunday morning worship, I was praying and asking God if wanting the Eucharist and Holy Communion so urgently and strongly was bad. One puts in as much routine as you can even in a situation when routine wasn't occurring. One of my routines on Sunday mornings was worship. We're people of habit; having my own worship with scriptures and songs was a natural for me.

"On this Sunday, I felt an incredible knowledge and infilling telling me wanting communion was not wrong, but I would not take communion in the traditional manner with the bread and wine for a long, long time.

"I still get goose bumps thinking about what happened days later. On Wednesday, I got a letter from the Franciscan Sisters, the Catholic mother house in Syracuse, New York. The envelope from the Sisters arrived, and in it was a little brochure with a prayer for spiritual communion. It was phenomenal to me and really wonderful to have my desire for communion acknowledged by God and to be reminded God's Holy Communion is only a prayer away."

Going Beyond Survival

"I was able to find peace and inner strength in spite of my captivity. I had a strong foundation built for me. Religion was a part of my family's everyday life, not just a Sunday morning thing. We had family devotions and bedtime prayer. It was real in my parents' life and when they managed crises. It wasn't something we talked about.

"During my captivity, I found I needed to pray a lot, and some of my prayers were not just for me and my fellow hostages, but for the strength and hope for my family and others back home."

We Must Move On . . .

"Finally, on January 20, 1981 the Iranians released us to American officials and we all came back to the US. How amazing to see the way people celebrated our homecoming. Enduring all those days in captivity was certainly trying, but it did not keep me from going abroad again. After some other overseas assignments, I went back to Washington, DC for a while since I had a house there. Later, I started taking courses at a Lutheran seminary in Gettysburg, Pennsylvania. I ended up earning a master of arts in religion, because questions arose during my individual studies I needed answers to.

"I still had to decide where to settle down for retirement. I ended up coming back to Waverly in Iowa. It is perfect; I like small towns. The college where I had studied and previously taught is here. I found a house I like. One sister lives in Waverly, and the other three sisters live within forty minutes. We're close, and that's really nice. We're enjoying each other's company a lot.

"I was semi-retired for a while, but then Wartburg College asked me back. I agreed to teach courses in theatre, religion, and also in communications because of my work as a public speaker.

"I settled into a very nice and comfortable life in Waverly, with good connections at the college. I enjoyed wonderful opportunities with congenial colleagues and the academic milieu. I was doing quite a bit of speaking initially, but I have cut back recently.

"When I speak, I try to give a message of faith and hope. Being a little part of this huge thing of faith and belief, and bringing this to people's attention in some way—translating it into something they can understand— is awfully important."

WOW

Words of Wisdom from Kate Koob

How to Endure . . . "I don't want the hostage crisis to define my life. We all endure crises and traumas. What have you been through? What have you survived?

"Any trauma, violence, or crisis seems unbearable and unending at the time. So, instead of focusing on the fear and impending violence of a kidnapping, I'd rather talk about how we get through it all.

"Again, what is your trauma: loneliness, broken marriage, assault, rape, loss of job, death of a family member, or illness of a friend? All of these, and other life struggles, are difficult to endure. We need to survive the crises, learn from them, grow from them, and when possible, share how we endured our crises in order to help others deal with theirs. We do this out of love.

"Love is stronger than anything else we know, except the grace of God. I personally know the grace of God empowers us to do a lot of things we think we can't do."

What Can Y O U Do Now?

"You've read my story and my WOWs—Words of Wisdom—now, what about you?

"Read as much as you can about what the State Department actually does. Check out their website: www.state.gov and read the book *Inside a U.S. Embassy* by Shawn Dorman. Then, figure out what you really want to do. Do you want to be a political officer or an economic officer? Do you want to deal with consular law? Do you want to do educational and cultural exchange? The next step is to take the Foreign Service entrance exam. You have no limit on the number of times you can take it. If you are interested and want, try during your junior year for practice, you can certainly do that and then take it again another time.

"The advice I was given I think is still very important: Read as widely as you possibly can and have as broad a background as you can. In your specialty, whether it's political science, economics, administration, or consular law, be as savvy as you can with it. Know you are in deep competition because in any given year, literally tens of thousands of people take the exam. You must have a real desire to do it.

"If you have the chance, talk to people in Foreign Service. Find out what they're doing, what they would recommend, and what's going on. You may be asked to talk about foreign policy issues, and you should be versed and at least familiar with what's going on in the world. Again, a wide breadth of reading, particularly of news stories, is paramount.

"When I was press attaché in Australia, I read five different papers every morning. Be conversant beyond the American media. You need a different look at how the rest of the world sees what's going on, and getting another perspective is critical.

"Besides having an interest and passing the Foreign Service exam, a couple of other things are needed. You must have openness and an acceptance of things being done in a different way. You're not going to last in the

Foreign Service very long if you can't give up the comforts of home. You must be able to adapt and have a genuine interest in learning and knowing how another part of the world lives and functions, well beyond just curiosity.

"Definitely, the interpersonal relationships are imperative—working well with a team, because you are a part of a team. When you're working in an embassy, the ambassador is in charge, but a whole lot of people are under him with significant responsibilities. You need to have good working relationships with everyone."

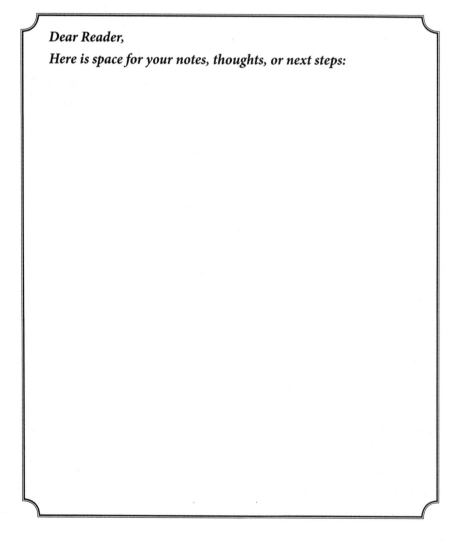

Dear Reader,
Here is space for your notes, thoughts, or next steps:

THE SOLDIER

MAJOR GENERAL CARL H. MCNAIR, JR., US ARMY (RET)

The United States Army named Major General (MG) Carl McNair, Jr. the first Chief of the aviation branch, a powerful and effective combat arm of the army. Gen. McNair earned the wings of a master aviator by flying more than 4,500 hours during his military career, with almost 1,500 of those hours in combat. His decorations include two awards of the Distinguished Service Medal, three awards of the Legion of Merit, four awards of the Distinguished Flying Cross, the Bronze Star with "V" device [denotes act of heroism], and the Air Medal with fifty-three clusters and "V" device. McNair contributed substantially to the advancement of women in the military, and he was not only named to the Army Aviation Hall of Fame, but also named a Distinguished Graduate of the US Military Academy at West Point, an honor bestowed on fewer than one hundred graduates.

This highly decorated soldier, airborne ranger, infantry aviator, and aerospace engineer built an exemplary military career and then retired after thirty-two years of service to commit his life to family, civic, and community service.

HOW DID HE DO THAT?

General Carl McNair praises his parents' teachings as having a profound effect on his way of life. General McNair's father, Carl McNair, Sr., served in the army until he left military life to become a civilian businessman. Much later, Carl, Jr. learned of another McNair family and army legacy which he shares with us.

Carl's mother, Hallie, exemplified attentiveness and compassion, serving as caregiver for each of her six siblings as well as her parents. He attributes his support of women in the military to observing his mother's entrepreneurial capabilities; she had opened and operated a kindergarten, and with her husband, a gasoline station and café.

A strong work ethic began early for Carl McNair when, at twelve years old, he delivered pharmacy medicines on his bicycle for a dollar a day. He says he enjoys coming to work still today and will continue as long as he can contribute to the well-being of our nation.

"I am Carl McNair. My parents' teachings, stellar educational opportunities to include matriculation at the US Military Academy at West Point, and a strong work ethic highlighted my rise to army general and countless active-duty service awards. Here's more of my story about how I did that . . ."

The Soldier's Story

The Foundation of Early Schooling

"Sincerely, my earliest schooling was fundamental, but much has changed since I began school. Education standards were not real high, especially in the south. The panhandle of Florida probably had some of the lowest-funded schools in the nation. The public schools where we lived were truly wanting, an example being classes with dual shifts. One group would go to school from eight in the morning to noon, and then we would put our books back in the desks. We would go home, and from one to five, someone else would come in, sit at the desk, and take the same books out. Although we were not people of means, my mom and dad felt we really should do better. Their resolution: private school, a nearby Catholic parochial school.

"My mother and daddy paid something like $25 or $30 a month out of our precious little funds for my sisters and me to attend Catholic school. At four years old, I started school in what we could call kindergarten. I would have turned five the end of September, but they didn't have enough kindergartners, so the nuns put me in first grade instead. When I reached twelfth grade, I was only fifteen.

> "MY CLASSMATES WOULD TALK ABOUT THEIR DADS FIGHTING IN THE PACIFIC. THEIR STORIES INSPIRED ME, AND I DEVELOPED AN INTEREST."

"Many students from the navy base attended the same Catholic school, exposing me to children whose dads were commanding submarines and aircraft carriers, or flying large float planes or fighter aircraft. My classmates would talk about their dads fighting in the Pacific. Their stories inspired me, and I developed an interest. All the other little boys would draw pictures of airplanes and ships, and that excited me. When airplanes flew over, many of the students would run over to the school windows and shout out, 'That's a PBY' [Patrol bomber] or 'That's an SNJ' [training craft]. They had knowledge to recognize aircraft from its sound that I had no feel for. I knew how to grow corn and pick tomatoes, but I didn't know anything about the military to speak of. I moved on into high school with a longing in the reaches of my mind to know more about flying and the military. Little did I know military opportunities would present themselves in my future."

Steps Toward a Change

"After the ninth grade, I moved to public school because it was very big, good, and offered a broader range of students. The Catholic high school had maybe fifty in the class, whereas the public high school had over 1,200 students, with four-hundred per class, and many more subjects to choose from. I, therefore, moved over in the tenth grade.

"When I reached my junior year, several of us took the traditional class trip to Washington, DC. In Washington, we visited the historic sites, including Arlington National Cemetery and the Capitol. When we went to meet Congressman Bob Sikes, who represented our home district in Florida for seventeen terms, he suggested we all take a copy of the pamphlets of West Point and Annapolis. I picked up a copy of both. The Air Force Academy wasn't founded until 1954.

"I had pretty much forgotten about those pamphlets until the summer before I would choose a college. Dad had coffee with a gentleman who asked, 'What's Carl going to do?' Dad told him, 'Carl is interested in going to Emory or Vanderbilt.' The gentleman said, 'Well, did he ever think of the academies?' I don't think daddy even knew much about West Point and Annapolis. He knew about being a private in the army, and lo and behold, he came home that night and said, 'Did you ever think about going to one of the academies? My friend said you might want to ask the Congressman about it.' I said, 'The only thing I know is I picked up a couple of books about the academies a few months ago.' I went in my room, found them on the bookshelf, and I started to read them a little more. I thought, 'Hey this doesn't sound too bad!'

"I typed the letter for my dad advising the Congressman of my interest in an academy appointment. Dad signed it with 'Carl is interested in Annapolis.' Of course, this was the genesis of it all. I still have copies of those letters, including the Congressman's return letter putting me in the queue. I was blessed to be picked for Annapolis, and it was announced in all the newspapers.

"Unfortunately, I wasn't old enough. You had to be seventeen by the day you entered the academy in July, so you would be twenty-one when you graduated four years later. The law requires regular officers be at least twenty-one. Although I satisfied all the physical, mental, academic, and aptitude requirements, I was simply not old enough. The Congressman, therefore, said to come back in a year."

A Preference for West Point

"Determined to continue my education, I went on to Emory University in Atlanta on an academic scholarship for pre-med. Life took another unexpected turn in my first year, when my dad experienced his second heart attack. I immediately went home to be with him since he was in critical care. When I went in and greeted daddy, he said, 'How did you do on your academy examinations?' I was supposed to take my exams for West Point in Atlanta that day, and he knew that. I said, 'Dad, I've done very well.' I truly think in his heart he preferred me to go to West Point than to be a doctor. He died later that very day. I took the balance of my entrance exams three months later at West Point, and, of course, I did pass them all.

"That's not to say I was the brightest turnip that fell off the truck, but I have always promised myself and my parents I would work as hard—or harder—than anybody in order to do the job as well—or better—than anyone else. I think I established that in most of the places where I served and where I studied. The competition proved substantial along my path. For example, in my squad and in my company at the academy, I had friends whose fathers were colonels and generals. I'd say, 'Wow, that's big. My daddy was a PFC, Private First Class Carl McNair, Sr.'"

Another McNair from a Long Time Ago

"As a matter of fact, many people—in the military and not—know the name 'McNair' because of Fort McNair in Washington, DC. The base's namesake, General Lesley J. McNair, served many decades prior to my father. Lesley McNair goes way, way back in my family in another generation. Gen. Lesley McNair graduated in the 1904 class of West Point, commanded ground forces in World War II, and at the time was the highest ranking soldier in US history killed on the field of battle.

"My ancestor's reputation preceded me at West Point. When I reached the academy, the instructors spent the first couple of weeks teaching us to drill, and our left foot was supposed to hit the ground on the heavy beat of the drum. Well, I was having a little trouble with it, and the upperclassmen asked me, 'Did you ever dance?' I replied, 'I danced, but not much.' One of the senior officers came over to where I was standing off to the side where the drill instructors were trying to help my foot hit when it was supposed to. The officer who approached us looked at my name tag, and said, 'McNair, that's a famous army name.' I said, 'Yes, sir.' We could only say three things: Yes sir, no sir, and no excuse, sir. I opted for, 'Yes, sir,' and he asked, 'Was your father in the Army?'

'Yes, sir.' He inquired, 'What was your father's rank?' 'Sir, he was a private first class, but the sergeant told him if he would re-enlist, they would promote him to corporal.'

"The lieutenant colonel went on to be a three-star general, and until I made general twenty-seven years later, he still thought I was teasing him. But, I was proud of my daddy, and frankly, I didn't know about THE General McNair then. I know a lot more about him now, though."

> "AS ALL SOLDIERS KNOW, THE ARMY DOESN'T PROMOTE YOU FOR WHAT YOU'VE DONE. SIMILARLY, INDUSTRY DOESN'T MAKE YOU A CHIEF EXECUTIVE OFFICER [CEO] FOR YOUR HAVING BEEN A CHIEF OPERATING OFFICER."

Dedication & Commitment: Taking on More

"I was thrilled to make general, yet challenged. As all soldiers know, the army doesn't promote you for what you've done. Similarly, industry doesn't make you a chief executive officer [CEO] for your having been a chief operating officer. They promote you in the army or make you the CEO based on your demonstrated potential and for what they believe you can and will do in the next position. I learned that early on. They want to find out all you can and will do.

"I had many chances to prove myself. In my first overseas assignment as a lieutenant in Taiwan, I was a pilot, only eighteen months out of training when I was selected as the senior pilot on the team, and the colonel's pilot for all missions. After a few months, the colonel, who had served in World War II said, 'You're only flying three or four days a week. In the afternoon, you can advise the ranger school. You can advise the honor guard, and I want you to get a band started, too.' I of course said, 'Yes, sir.' I had friends at Fort Benning in the ranger school who sent me training material. I also knew people in the honor guard in Washington, DC who helped me with drill routines, and people in the band back in America who would provide me sheet music. The next thing I knew, I was doing those other things, too, and I enjoyed it. I didn't mind being asked, as I had to ask a lot as well.

"I would never ever ask anybody to do anything I would not do, if I had the time and capability. This philosophy applied to flying missions, as well. I never asked anyone to fly more than I would fly. In my company during the Vietnam conflict, we flew literally thousands of hours of combat, got shot at and shot up, even shot down on occasion. I could not have faced my troops every morning when we took off if I had not flown as much, or more, as they had in the same fight, or volunteered for the same hazardous missions. With that commitment, I felt good about myself, and I felt good about those under my command. As a result, my pilots flew better, and we fought harder for each other."

Making a Choice

"Upon returning from advisory duty in Taiwan, I received orders to go to graduate school at the same time that the commanding general of Fort Benning, Georgia, was selected to serve as the chief of the military advisory group in Taiwan. While screening for the general's aide, the personnel officer at Benning noticed I had recently returned from Taiwan. Because I could speak some Mandarin Chinese and had experience in Taiwan, it was suggested I delay graduate school to be the general's aide.

"I felt I was at a crossroad, so I went to a colonel with whom I had served in Taiwan, and who was then in a senior position at Benning. I simply asked, 'What do you think, sir?' He was a World War II veteran and very astute. He said, 'You know being a general's aide is a great opportunity. You get to wear a little different brass.' 'But,' he added, 'never turn down a school. Who knows, you go away for two years, and they cut out sending people to school. Anything could happen. If you really want to get the graduate training, go now. You can be an aide sometime later if you really want to be an aide.' Consequently, I chose school. It was a sacrifice because a general's aide is recognized as one chosen from among a select group of officers. By declining the aide's position and later having the aerospace engineering degree, I found myself briefing top officials at the Pentagon and, even in the junior grade of captain, attending meetings in the executive office building of the White House and the office of the Secretary of Defense. The long hours and unending days at the Pentagon led to my earning the Legion of Merit very early in my career. The opportunity to broaden my education proved to be the right decision for me."

"I FOUND MYSELF BRIEFING TOP OFFICIALS AT THE PENTAGON AND EVEN IN THE JUNIOR GRADE OF CAPTAIN, ATTENDING MEETINGS IN THE EXECUTIVE OFFICE BUILDING OF THE WHITE HOUSE."

Answering the Call: The COBRA Helicopter

"During the mobilization of the Vietnam conflict, I again served for a time at the Pentagon. Again, I worked all hours, all days. I was at work one Saturday morning all alone in an office usually staffed with fifteen officers during the regular work week. The hot line to the colonel's office rang. I went in, answered the call, and found myself speaking to the assistant secretary of the army responsible for research, development, and acquisition systems. He said, 'Carl, I've just had a call from the secretary of the army, Stanley Resor. We must have the final list for all the priority requirements for Vietnam by eight o'clock tonight to Secretary Resor so the list can get to the White House for congressional action. He has to leave tonight at eight o'clock to attend a formal function with his wife. If we don't have the gunship requirements for the new COBRA [army attack helicopter] to him by eight, we can forget the COBRA.' The assistant secretary continued, 'Can you get everyone together to work on this?' 'Yes, sir,' I replied.

"I immediately started making calls. I reached the two-star general who handled requirements, who was also in his office that Saturday. He came down, as did our deputy in R&D, and the vice-chief of staff of the army. We all went into the assistant secretary's office to start the required work. The vice-chief of staff was at the blackboard writing down numbers. The assistant secretary was over at his desk figuring things. We put the charts and letter together, and at 7:30 p.m. the assistant secretary sent me to deliver the packet. I walked up to Secretary Resor's office at ten minutes to eight. His wife was sitting on the couch in a gown, tapping her high heels saying, 'Stanley, we've got to go. We've got to go.' He was in a tuxedo and told her, 'I have to sign this letter so it can go up to Mr. [Robert] McNamara [Secretary of Defense] tonight.'

"What would have happened had we not assembled that small group that day or were unable to take the assignment and complete it? We might not have had the COBRA, and the helicopter was critical to America in Vietnam. I came to work that Saturday to work on other duties related to my priority projects, but I was fortunate to have been there and to have answered when the call came."

No Atheists in the Foxhole

"I would return to the field, to combat. In that environment, you never know what you're going to face, thus faith in yourself, your troops, and your God are vital elements. I will tell you, and you've heard it before, and I'm a living witness, 'There are no atheists in the foxhole.'

"In my helicopter company in the first eight months of combat in 1968 in Vietnam—during one of the most intense combat periods of the war—I lost some aircraft to enemy fire, but far more costly, I lost eight soldiers, two full crews of two aviators, gunners, and a crew chief in each. At the memorial services for those young men, I praised them and prayed for them with tears in my eyes and a lump in my throat. Losing them was tough because I lived with them, fought with them, and even helped recover their remains from the field of battle. Ironically, I was the old man, and I was only thirty-four. These guys were eighteen, nineteen, twenty, and twenty-one.

"At times when we were flying in the middle of the dark of night, eleven or twelve o'clock, over the jungles of South Vietnam, we would ask ourselves, 'If my engine quit now, what would happen? Would I die in the jungle or get captured and become a POW?'

"Coming back one night late, that old engine just kept humming. I had already flown ten to twelve hours, as I recall. We landed, put the bird to bed, got up, and left about six the next morning for another mission. This time, I took a division commander and his key staff as my crew inserted troops into an area taken by the Vietcong and North Vietnamese. We put in about twenty lifts and about 200 troops, who immediately made contact with the enemy. I was flying the same helicopter I had the night before. It probably had five more hours on the engine since the night before, and it quit cold in mid-flight. I mean, we went down right in the middle of the bad guys. We set up a perimeter and, after a few minutes, a US Air Force rescue helicopter heard our mayday call and came to pick us up. A crew member shouted, 'It's a blue helicopter, sir.' I said, 'I don't care what color it is, we're getting in it!' I had sent all our own helos back to rearm and refuel during a lull in battle. If the engine failure had happened the night before, we would likely all have been dead. All we could say was, 'Wow. Amazing!' So, no, there are no atheists in the foxhole."

Women in the Army and in Aviation

"The foxhole is perhaps about to change, but the pilot seats changed many years ago as women entered the military. When I arrived in Fort

Rucker, Alabama in 1974 as a young colonel, to command the aviation brigade, I had six battalions of about 6,000 troops, and the first women had just come into flight training. I had a WAC [Women's Army Corps] company located across the parking lot from my headquarters building. A WAC captain was the commanding officer, and all the women soldiers lived in the same building under a female because, gee, how could a male commander have women in his barracks, or how could a female officer inspect men's quarters?

"Beyond this, however, the uniqueness of all the female soldiers in the same unit was a major attraction for the male soldiers. In the afternoons around five o'clock, the cars would start pulling up to the women's detachment and the male soldiers would be sitting on the fenders waiting for the female soldiers so they could attend athletic events or other activities on post.

"The magnetism of the women's unit was amazing, but in 1975 the army directed all women be integrated into their own units. The novelty was over. We put them together—the two women who were in the band moved to the band barrack, and the ones who were engineers went to the engineers building. We experienced far fewer problems once we integrated the women with the men.

"I congratulated the first women who completed flight training, and pinned the wings on their uniforms. The military services were late in realizing the need for equality. However, women were ready, and knew they were ready, long before the military changed the regulations and statutes to accommodate them."

Undergraduate Observation

"Reflecting on women in the military reminds me of a conversation I had when I went to visit my daughter in college at William & Mary. She introduced me to the president of her sorority, who immediately said to me, 'General, I understand you run a flying school in the army. Tell me, do you have any women in the school?' This was a very mature college senior. I said, 'As a matter of fact, we do. Right now, we have about twenty-eight women in flight training, and we're taking more every day.' Then she asked, 'How are they doing?' I shook my finger at her and said, 'You'd be surprised at how well they're doing.' She then said, 'No, I wouldn't be surprised. You might be.' That stuck with me ever since.

"The women have done masterfully and equally well. That's why I say folks like Laura Richardson and Anne Macdonald, our first two female general officer aviators, and those of other branches who went on to become general officers, are truly to be admired and respected. I could mention many others, and I know we'll have more."

From General to Captain of Industry

"Men and women alike who serve in the military would give our lives for our comrades. I can say I love the army as I love my family and my own life. But while I love the military, I retired earlier than I planned because my wife suffered a catastrophic stroke at age fifty, at the peak of my career. But I have remained committed to the US Army and still deeply involved through military organizations. Thank goodness, since I retired in 1987, I have also had opportunities to work for a number of companies.

"One of the companies you're probably familiar with is DynCorp. Joining them in 1990, I became president of DynCorp's smallest division, which emerged as its largest unit with significant growth over nine years. I especially enjoy that I can assist in oversight and management for private companies and non-profits. One never stops learning and I consider a perfect day to be one in which I learn something new and contribute to the growth of others and to emerging companies or charities. I haven't been in a position of receiving advice in quite some time, and most of those who had advised and mentored me through my career have passed on. They certainly left me a legacy. They taught me most of what I try to practice today. I must also say I turn to prayer an awful lot. Certainly, whatever successes or goals I may have achieved, they were not earned by me alone, but in partnership with a higher power."

WOW

Words of Wisdom from Gen. Carl McNair

Leadership... "The first thing one must have is a willingness to follow. We must be willing to follow before we can lead.

"In the military, certainly, you have to be able to take orders and follow those orders. In the military, leaders say, 'We tear you down to build you up.' Some come from high positions in life, and others come from very humble beginnings, proud but humble. They all have to start at the same place.

"I had classmates whose fathers were four-star generals. We've had West Pointers whose fathers later became President of the United States. You have every class of society, almost every race who attend the academies. You also have people from many foreign countries, such as Mexico or the Philippines, as well, who go on to become presidents of their own countries or heads of their armies. Your chosen path can take you far if you can first follow.

"The follow-to-lead philosophy goes beyond the military. We see it in families where often a child will follow his mother or father around, and then sooner or later, the child leads other children around.

"Certainly, if you're going to become a Christian, you have got to follow Christ first. Then you can lead other people to Christ."

Work Ethic... "I think you have to be willing to go the extra mile, exert the extra ounce of energy, and invoke the full measure of devotion. I don't want to speak against anybody, but you have those who say they want to work eight to five. Man, they bolt at five o'clock! They will get paid, and they may even get promoted to a certain level. But frankly, in the military and in private industry, organizational leaders select the top performers from those who go the extra mile.

"The bottom line is production. When I say production in combat, I see production as the soldier who goes up the hill the farthest and goes up the fastest in order to protect, save lives, and accomplish missions. In the business world—I promise you—you can be the nicest person, the best liked, the most athletic, or perhaps even the brightest, but you have to prove you are critical to your company's performance and mission accomplishment."

Life Decisions . . . "You must learn to make your decisions on your own. On some of the military elimination boards, I'd sit listening to and watching a bright young cadet who was not performing well and about to be discharged. I would ask, 'If you don't like it here at the Academy, why are you here?' Many times the answer was, 'Well, sir, really I came because my parents wanted me to.' I'd say, 'That's not the answer.' That's not the best way."

What Can **YOU** Do Now?

"You've read my story and my WOWs—Words of Wisdom—now, what about you?

"I will say to you the sage advice given to me: 'Never turn down a school; never turn down something which will advance you.' Education is paramount. You've got to consider that as fundamental. I don't recommend a general degree. Work on a specific discipline within your major, and the more technical, sometimes the better. Whether you like it or not, when you apply for a job—even with a degree—if you don't have the specified disciplines, chances are the computer will throw your resume out before you have a chance to see the interviewer. Additionally, where you stand in your class does matter. You don't have to be number one, but you don't want to be last either.

"Now, let's talk money. Any man or woman today can get an education if they truly want to, no excuses. I'm not saying to get the big loans. Did you ever think about going to one of the smaller schools? Sometimes, they'll pay *you*. So, you might not have to have a lot of money.

"High school guidance counselors and college advisors can be very helpful to you. An additional resource referred to me is the College Board, which you can research further at www.collegeboard.com.

"You can also have the military pay for your education. Each branch of the military has recruiting information on its website. Many cities have walk-in recruitment offices. You can even explore ROTC and Junior ROTC programs. Additionally, if you have an excellent high school record, you can consider the military academies. Check their websites or with your congressional representative for requirements.

"Advice you can use and pass on to anyone: Think ahead. Evaluate all options. Plan responsibly. Commit totally. Act smartly. Follow through completely. Keep the faith. Relish achievement. Lead others to do the same."

Dear Reader,

Here is space for your notes, thoughts, or next steps:

THE MINISTER
REV. JOHNNY PARKER

Johnny Parker is an author, speaker, life coach, counselor, consultant, and ministry leader. His clients include his hometown team of the Washington Redskins, other NFL teams, and professional athletes in the NBA, PGA, and WNBA. Having been affiliated with the First Baptist Church of Glen Arden (FBCG) for many years, Johnny currently serves as director of spiritual care, where he leads FBCG's counseling, life coaching, and men's ministries.

HOW DID HE DO THAT?

Johnny Parker sought refuge in the suburbs of Washington, DC after growing up in the Queens borough of New York as an isolated youngster with low self-esteem. He left that life behind, traveling south to attend college. He graduated, went on to complete seminary, and as he continued to grow and develop himself, doors opened. Paths took him to stadiums filled with hundreds, behind the microphone of radio stations, to one-on-one counseling sessions, Bible study classes, mega-church leadership, and to the church pulpit. Much of this work came Johnny's way unsought and unsolicited.

"First and foremost, I am a committed husband and father. My life experiences, earning a doctorate in strategic leadership, and my earlier education have equipped me to consult with corporations, often their CEOs, and other high-profile leaders. I counsel with or urge my clients, fellow worshippers, friends, and family to have flourishing relationships at home, school, or work. Here's more of my story about how I do that . . ."

The Minister's Story

Crushed Grapes Experiences

"I really believe, as I have heard one man say, 'God takes our crushed grapes and makes wine.' We never know the wine we're becoming when we feel crushed like grapes. Now I know a lot of what I experienced in my youth was a crushing grapes experience. This is the sensitive part: I don't know how to talk about it. I haven't much. When I was young—about nine or ten years old—my parents divorced. Thankfully, my parents have remarried, but at the time, the breakup, and all leading to the breakup, had a strong effect on me.

"I know that time of my life and those experiences really marked me. I know I had this pain, and I was working through it. Life made me want to be a psychologist. I wanted to do something to help people in relationships, and to help families not just stay together, but stay together in a healthy, wholesome, and fulfilling life.

"For a long time as a youngster I was extremely insecure. I didn't have a lot of confidence because of distractions with my parents' issues. I didn't feel I was really given the emotional care and tending I needed. As a result, I had this question mark over my heart in terms of my identity: 'Who was I?'

"I was hungry for attention and affirmation. Those needs were huge. The junior high years were very, very hard—very, very difficult. Academically in school I always did fairly well, but I definitely had gaps in my learning and in my abilities due to the hurt I was feeling.

"I didn't realize the effect of the home life then, but one thing I do remember was my reaction regarding having a family of my own. I wanted my future family to be everything opposite of what I was experiencing. I wanted to be married, have kids one day, and have fun, laugh, and do things I thought healthy families ought to do.

"All I can think of is I turned inward. I was extremely jealous. I had no sense of identity—I remember that. I would take on the persona of the individual who seemed to be the go-to person, the person who got the attention. I would try to become that person. I had no sense of my own personality. I remember not feeling worthy of anything. I felt like I was getting close to the edge in terms of living, and allowing the streets to dictate my life. The streets called for me, and I felt myself tempted to go toward them.

"I got in trouble in junior high and early in high school, trying to gain attention from the peer group I hung out with. I found myself in the wrong place at the wrong time. I didn't commit a crime, but I landed in a courtroom when I was thirteen. What a big mess.

"My family knew, and they were all praying. I was praying, too! Everyone prayed and hoped everything would work out. How funny I prayed, because I didn't know God, but I was scared. I figured God was a good one to turn to in a situation like this. I didn't know how to pray; I only knew the child's bedtime prayer, 'Now I lay me down to sleep . . .'"

Beginning to Turn Around

"I began to observe different things in my surroundings. I lived with my grandparents for some of my high school years. They had been married for more than forty years. Even though my father was gone, my grandfather was extremely faithful to whatever he did, very committed. My grandparents were very religious, and my grandfather was a pastor of a church. When I did go to church, I went to his church. He had a very strong influence on my life. I would see my grandfather praying every morning and night. He had the Christian radio station on, and I would hear their music. All of that was going on.

"When I was in the 11th grade, I noticed a different group of kids. They seemed like they had joy and were positive. They were doing constructive things, while I was doing all these negative things. I wanted what they had, although I did not realize just yet what they had was their religion. They knew the Lord.

"We had a Gospel choir at school, and those kids were all a part of this group. They were a fun, clean, healthy-looking group—the kind of group every parent would want their kid to be a part of. I just wanted to hang out with them. I wasn't trying to be religious. I viewed church and Christianity as something for old people—anyone over thirty-five was old to me at that time. I thought people really only thought seriously about God when they were old and ready to die. I hadn't seen anyone who was excited about God in my age group—not until I saw this Gospel choir.

> "I DIDN'T KNOW WHAT THEY KNEW ABOUT JESUS, BUT I SAID, 'WELL, I LIKE THEIR LIFESTYLE.' I WANTED WHAT THEY HAD. THEY SEEMED TO HAVE AUTHENTIC JOY, AND THEY SEEMED TO BE HAPPY."

"I didn't know what they knew about Jesus, but I said, 'Well, I like their lifestyle.' I wanted what they had. They seemed to have authentic joy, and they seemed to be happy. I started hanging out with the choir, and one of the young ladies in the group knew the kind of lifestyle I lived. She told me about a relationship with Christ. I was receptive; I was desperate. I wanted something to change in my life because I didn't like my path and my pain.

"I can't remember how exactly, but she asked me, 'Do you know Jesus Christ?' I said, 'No.' She told me I needed to pray, confess to Him I was a sinner, ask Him to forgive me, and ask Him to come into my life. I went straight home and prayed. I prayed to ask Jesus into my life. That was December of 1978. I was sixteen, and after my prayer, I began to feel my first sense of identity."

Focused on Learning

"I became hungry to read the Bible. I would take the Bible to school, and I would put it on my desk. I was bold, and I didn't care what anyone thought. I couldn't get enough of reading the scriptures; I had this insatiable appetite. I would hurry home, get my homework done, and boom, I would be in the Bible studying and reading—reading, reading, and reading.

"My junior year in high school, I was thinking, 'OK, I know I am going to college.' I was now clear on why I wanted to go to college and what I wanted to study. I wanted to study the Bible. I wanted to be a theologian. I didn't know what a theologian did, but I wasn't going to college to make big money. I was going to college because I was passionate about God. I went to the extreme. I turned radical about my faith. I wanted to go to a place with only Christians. I wanted everybody around me to be Christian, and I looked in the college handbook and found a Bible college in the DC area where I could study theology and prepare for a life of ministry.

"We had family in Maryland, and I believed that connection was God making a way for me. Back then this area was so different from New York. It felt rural to me, and I liked it. It was quiet, unlike New York.

"When I was in college, my vision for myself was to become a Christian counselor, get married, work with a church, and teach Bible classes. I didn't have a view of my life being as large and impactful as it has become. I didn't, I really didn't. I never even saw myself as a speaker. In fact, I avoided courses in college with speaking since I was petrified of speaking!"

From the Heart

"As I started working with and counseling people, I began to realize I had an ability to help people. In counseling sessions I heard patterns of how people got angry or depressed, and I assisted them with changing those behaviors and reactions. I had a passion for helping people and recognized I could coach them or comfort them—and sometimes confront them, whatever it took to get them to turn their lives around. The more I had these one-on-one experiences where I could see positive changes in people and they could see it in themselves, the more I wanted to go public in order to achieve change in greater numbers. I felt I had to put my fear of speaking aside so I could reach more people. I wanted people to be free. I wanted them to have joy. I couldn't keep my compassion and ability to help to myself. If speaking in large groups would help more people in a shorter period of time, then that's what I had to do.

"I started speaking to larger audiences, and became aware I could clearly do this. I spoke from my heart, and I noticed people were listening. People were connecting with what I was saying and making changes. Their success was my success, and I started getting more calls to speak."

> "IN COUNSELING SESSIONS I HEARD PATTERNS OF HOW PEOPLE GOT ANGRY OR DEPRESSED, AND I ASSISTED THEM WITH CHANGING THOSE BEHAVIORS AND REACTIONS."

Unsolicited Blessings

"Rather early in my ministry work, I was invited to be a part of a couple of different national ministries. One of the ministries held huge rallies, bringing in thousands of worshippers and others who came seeking change in their lives. The other ministry, *Family Life Today*, reached millions through its radio network, conferences, and missions outreach. McLean Bible Church in Fairfax County, Virginia then asked me to join its staff. I was the first African-American minister at McLean Bible. I didn't ask to join either organization, and I didn't pursue them. I was minding my business and speaking from my heart, and doors of opportunity would fly open.

"Those opportunities were all God's doing, no question, absolutely, because I didn't seek those platforms. Is this the way it should happen for everyone? I don't know, but that's what happened for me. I feel like I absolutely see God in my path."

Church Leadership and Personal Development

"At this moment, I see my life at almost two extremes. I stay busy with and am thrilled with my ministry work at First Baptist Church of Glen Arden and with my vocation as counselor and life coach. At the other end of the spectrum, I regularly spend time in solitude to renew myself, hear from God, and to listen to my heart. I call it soul-scaping. I have a place in the woods where I can go and reflect and write in my journal. I look at my own emotional weeds and work on pulling them out of myself. This time of quiet has become fundamental to my success. This I know I must do to be the husband, father, and servant of the world I want to be."

WOW

Words of Wisdom from Johnny Parker

Self Truth . . . "I want people to know if we are to live our lives to the fullest, we have to live from the inside-out. By that I mean we can't be driven by the externals and the appearances. We must examine what's in our heart. I think living externally, according to what *appears* to be successful, is easier. I just feel like I always want to call on people to be authentic: to be authentic with ourselves, in marriages, and other relationships—really with everything they do."

Time Alone . . . "We must take time to process, to be alone with ourselves. Our hearts have so many distractions today. Life is moving fast, and we want quick fixes. We want a microwave life because we don't want to take the time to really sit and be alone with our hearts in solitude. But we need to get to a place alone, away from distractions, and listen. We need to be intentional about what we're hearing from inside ourselves and what we want to put into practice. I think time alone is absolutely critical."

Heart Questions . . . "As I mentioned earlier, I try to fit alone time in once a week. I try to get away to a quiet place to think and process, to order my steps, to order my life, to not be afraid to ask myself the hard questions of my heart as a husband, as a father, and as a professional. If I am going to be successful and live my life to the fullest, I must have solitude. I don't think this is just true of me. I think this is the truth, and we've got to do it. We've got to have private time, time to be one-on-one with ourselves.

"I always come back to that message: How do you take time to look at your heart, to live your life from the inside out? Over and over, we have to ask ourselves: 'What dreams, talents, gifts inside me, if not developed, would be a loss to the world? What am I avoiding and why? What would I do if I were not afraid? What gives me life, renews me, and refreshes me? Why is a particular thing or person important to me? What's motivating me? What makes me angry?' These kinds of heart questions can free us if we address them."

Accountability . . . "Yet, we still must enter into a kind of community with other people so we have accountability. I am bothered when I hear reports about infidelity or child abuse. I'm thinking that didn't just happen; it was an inside-out kind of a deal. Someone got away from his heart. As I said, I'm always trying to help people understand who they are privately, because who you are inside affects everything you do on the outside."

What Can YOU Do Now?

"You've read my story and my WOWs—Words of Wisdom—now, what about you?

"These following steps you need to take in order. First, work in ministry or as a life coach will require you to grow personally, to grow your own self-awareness. You can achieve growth in self-awareness by journaling about God, your thoughts about your life, and your relationships. The more you take time to self-reflect, you will understand the benefits of reflection, and that will allow you to support others in doing the same.

"Second, consider how you can leave people better off than you found them. Identifying and using your own gifts, skills, and talents as you work with people is important. Referring back to step one, again, the more you self-reflect, the more you can assist others.

"Third, cultivate a love for reading. Read a lot and spend some time with people who are smarter than you. In other words, find books on specific topics you are hearing as recurring themes of interest to you. Take classes, go to conferences, and attend workshops from people who are respected and credible in their fields or in a specific discipline. None of us is in this alone. I like to say, 'A healthy me makes a healthy we.'

"I invite you to look at the resources at www.johnnyparker.com and at www.fbcglenarden.org."

Dear Reader,
Here is space for your notes, thoughts, or next steps:

The Corporate Executive
Sherman Parker

S herman Parker was one of two African-American students in the 1960s selected to desegregate King George County schools in Virginia. Parker endured the experience, continued his education, obtained a job at a Fortune 500 company, and became an executive for the Fortune 500 Xerox Corporation.

How Did He Do That?

Sherman recognizes the work ethic of his parents and grandparents as having a positive impact on him. The four of them set the example on a daily basis, and they afforded Sherman and his brother opportunities—like a college education—not given to their father or mother, nor their grandparents. Not only did Sherman's parents make sure he had an education, Sherman says the very best thing they did was to pray for him. Though he studied and worked hard, he acknowledges others did as well. But because of his family's prayers and God's grace, he was tapped for promotions beyond goals he had set for himself. He said he finally learned to pray and study God's Word consistently himself, and as he did, the blessings just kept coming. He credits his family's prayers, his own journey into Bible study and prayer, and finally, yes, his hard work and life experiences for his corporate ascent.

"I am Sherman Parker. I give all the credit for any success in my life to God. I am the beneficiary of prayers and love of my family. One of my favorite scriptures is Proverbs 3:5,6: 'Trust in the Lord with all thine heart; and lean not unto thine own understanding. In all thy ways acknowledge him, and he shall direct thy paths.' Here's some of my story on how He shaped my life . . ."

The Corporate Executive's Story

A Life-Changing Experience

"Many years ago, in 1963, I was selected to desegregate the public school system in King George County, Virginia. I remember sitting at the dinner table when my parents told me I would be one of two Negro students to desegregate the schools in King George County. I was fourteen at the time and remember snatches of a dinner table conversation when my father announced I would be going to King George High School in the fall. During the summer, I put the impending change out of my mind. I ignored the fact that a huge adjustment was coming. Maybe this was my way of coping with my uneasiness. A week before school began, I started getting really nervous, but I didn't feel I could tell my parents I didn't want to go. They were not going to change their minds.

"The first day of school was like no other for me. Some people wanted a police car to take me to school, but instead, my father took responsibility. A crowd of angry students and their parents stood on the steps leading to the school doors. My dad got out of the car and started walking. About midway up the steps, my father grabbed my hand. He walked us straight toward the crowd and when we got to them, the crowd parted.

"The walk up those stairs was an unforgettable experience, one I still admire and respect my father for, who was only in his mid-thirties at the time. My father was holding my hand the first day of school, and I know God was holding his.

> "THE WALK UP THOSE STAIRS WAS AN UNFORGETTABLE EXPERIENCE, ONE I STILL ADMIRE AND RESPECT MY FATHER FOR, WHO WAS ONLY IN HIS MID-THIRTIES AT THE TIME. MY FATHER WAS HOLDING MY HAND THE FIRST DAY OF SCHOOL, AND I KNOW GOD WAS HOLDING HIS."

"King George High School, where whites went to school, was so different from Ralph Bunche, the school for blacks. We had studied and played with other children from our neighborhood and had nurturing African-American teachers at Ralph Bunche. Prejudice and mistreatment were rampant for me when I started at King George High School. Racism was everywhere—even in the classroom. I had been an excellent student, but during the first year of desegregation, my grades suffered. Part of the reason my grades fell was due to my own nervousness, but the prejudice and discrimination toward me from students didn't help. Some of the teachers discriminated, too. Sometimes I just didn't get credit for the higher grades I had earned. I had all white teachers, and I remember one teacher in particular who was very mean to me. She would call me names. She once said, 'Negroes take longer to figure things out.' She was real rude, especially to be saying such things to a fourteen-year-old child. 'I don't want you here. I don't know why you're in this classroom,' she would say.

"Thank God, all teachers were not like her. One positive example was an English teacher, Eldon Cooke, who took an interest in me and helped me. Most of the time, though, the situation was pretty ugly. As tough as the classroom environment was, sometimes the hallways were just plain scary. I couldn't go to the bathroom because students were waiting to fight me. I couldn't go to the cafeteria for they were waiting to tease me. I couldn't get a drink from the water fountain; I didn't dare turn my back on them.

"After a period of time, I experienced not only the bad, but the good. In my mind, an angel stepped in. This angel was in the person of a brawny football player named Joe Hague. Joe heard the other white students jeering me in study hall one day. He asked the taunters why they were doing it, and then he said, 'Why don't you just leave him alone?' Two great things happened after: Those students didn't harass me anymore, and Joe became my friend. I always had an angel, and I believe God is always there for us. He always sends someone to protect His own. What an important thing to understand. I knew about the Lord then, but I didn't understand all His provisions. As I look back over my life, I can see how the Lord was always providing for me."

Varied Educational Influences

"I made it through the transition to desegregated schools and graduated from King George High School in 1967. Of course, completing high school laid the foundation for any success I would have. In spite of my parents' limited formal education, they provided the opportunity for me to go to college. My father, a laborer for the federal government, and my mother, a domestic, both made sacrifices for my brother and me monetarily and personally. I remember one time my brother and I were playing around and missed the bus to our elementary school. My mother was off that day, but my dad had the car at work. My mom said 'Come on, I will walk you to school.' We had to walk down a dirt road and cross a creek known to have snakes in it, and my mother was ghastly afraid of snakes! She didn't even like riding by the creek when we were in a car, but she walked us three miles to school. I remember turning around and watching her begin to walk back down the dirt road by herself. She was so brave, and that was a defining moment because she really placed the emphasis on commitment—going to school and doing what you're supposed to do—no matter what."

Beyond College

"As far as my parents were concerned, attending college was a must for their children, something neither of them got to do, and they made the importance they placed on getting as much education as possible very clear to us. Unlike my parents, I was able to get an undergraduate college degree and also a graduate degree. Some of my college experiences and those early days of desegregation at King George High School helped me learn to cope on my own when I needed to, and how to be content by myself when others were not around. This time of isolation prepared me for the corporate world, though I didn't know it at the time. Corporate America can be extremely lonely, especially for African-American men, since not many attain the upper echelons of Fortune 500 companies.

"When I traveled across the country or internationally, I felt all alone, but not nearly as alone as I felt when I was the only black male in the halls of King George High School. Amazingly, the desegregation experiences helped prepare me for the extensive travel I would do as a part of my job. I didn't and still don't have this need to meet coworkers or friends at a bar. The Lord

"CORPORATE AMERICA CAN BE EXTREMELY LONELY, ESPECIALLY FOR AFRICAN-AMERICAN MEN, SINCE NOT MANY ATTAIN THE UPPER ECHELONS OF FORTUNE 500 COMPANIES."

was preparing me then for what I needed. At one time, I had an international job and had to travel to Japan. Many times, I was the only American in the room, but I wasn't bothered by it, other than the language barrier.

"I worked very hard . . . I had learned a strong work ethic, especially from my father and my grandfather. Besides my education and the experiences that went along with it, I attribute a strong work ethic to my career advancements. Again, I was the beneficiary of what others did. I watched my father and grandfather and how they worked. We worked outside all the time. I learned a lot about life from my father. His father lived next door to him and refused to come into the 20th century. What I mean is my grandfather plowed with horses and raised chickens and cows! I felt like I lived in two eras. My grandfather had a very strong work ethic and did his best. As for my dad, he would work his job, come home, and work in the garden. He constantly provided for us, but he was also always 'present.' He never missed a PTA meeting. Sometimes, he worked shift work. He would take us to church on his way to work and made sure someone could take us home. He had more influence than I knew at the time, but he did put that same commitment to family into me. My father's expectation was for me to attain a college education, and my requirement was for my children to attain at least an advanced degree in graduate school, which they have all done."

On the Job

"I have given my best during my thirty-five plus years at Xerox. Early in my career I was an administrative manager supporting the corporate sales organization. I remember not being asked or viewed as capable for any opportunities in the major account sales organization. Now, I have led for thirteen years the public sector major account sales organization that is responsible for large account sales to government customers in the United States for the corporation. As a vice president in our public sector operations, I have more than surpassed my goal. Still, I can't emphasize enough how my career advancements came because God provided.

"Whether in my work life or personally, I don't hold a grudge or remind the doubters and cynics of what they might have said or done to try to discourage me or hold me back, because God handles those situations, too.

"As an executive at Xerox, I am thankful to be in a position where I can help others and where I can demonstrate responsibility. In general, my thoughts for those who have attained executive level status in a corporation are, 'We are probably not as good as we think we are on our best days, and we're probably not as bad as we think we are on our worst days. We have just been blessed, blessed to have this level of responsibility, authority, power, and compensation.' We have to ask ourselves, 'Why are we here, and others are not?' As African-Americans at this level in a company, we especially need to be on the watch to build the bridge over for other people."

WOW
Words of Wisdom from Sherman Parker

Life Lessons . . . "I learned many lessons: One, I gained coping skills. Secondly, I came to understand we are not alone. Thirdly, I know now to work hard in spite of tough situations. I also learned life is not always fair, but we still have to be. Because others helped me, I have an obligation to help others."

Faith . . . "Most importantly, I have learned what works best is what is found in *The Holy Bible*. Like I said before, Proverbs teaches us to trust God completely, and the same can work for you. In religious circles you hear people say, 'God is never late; He shows up right on time.' Well, I have learned it is not a matter of God showing up. God is always present. Rather, I know we need to show up! We need to choose to study His Word. Then we can be the ones to show courage, and if necessary, choose to walk through the jeering crowds. We can be the ones to speak out and reach out to help others."

What Can YOU Do Now?

"You've read my story and my WOWs—Words of Wisdom—now, what about you?

"If you want to work in private industry or really hold down any job, I say to you what I have said to and tried to instill in my children. First, education is very important. My parents wanted me to get my college degree. I wanted my children, now all responsible working adults, to get advanced degrees. The world has become so much more competitive than it used to be. Therefore, learning another language would be very helpful. As I travel the world, I see the expanse of competition. Most people from other countries speak English, and more of us would be well-served to learn other languages. You can use the second language to your benefit if you have that knowledge.

"Finally, do your best and let God do the rest because 'all things work for the good of those who love the Lord and are called according to His purpose.'" (Romans 8:28)

Dear Reader,

Here is space for your notes, thoughts, or next steps:

The Entrepreneurs
Jack and Magee Spencer

Jack & Magee Spencer are successful entrepreneurs who have made millions in the multi-level product marketing industry. For over thirty-five years, they have mentored hundreds personally, and thousands more in group settings, resulting in hundreds of independent businesses throughout the US and in other countries.

How Did They Do That?

Jack combined encouragement from his parents, mentoring from basketball coaches, and what he learned about the benefit of continuous practice to create a successful business and family life.

Magee emulated her mother's kindness and work ethic and interjected her own straightforward but humorous personality to add successful business woman to her résumé as homemaker, teacher, mother, and friend.

"Operating as Spencer Enterprises, we have grown our network marketing business successfully for more than thirty years, and have been happily married even longer. We have business teams throughout the US and in other countries, and travel widely to speak at business and leadership functions. Here's more of our story about how we did that . . ."

The Entrepreneurs' Story

Getting Started

(Jack) "We began earnestly believing if we followed the business plan and core business steps the way they were presented to us, we could have a better lifestyle for ourselves and our family. That really pushed me.

"I then had to break it down to what I needed to do on a daily basis. Basically, I had to think back and remember where I had been successful before, and that was as a basketball player in high school and on college scholarship. As an athlete, I knew about passion, and I knew about working hard to win. In basketball, I practiced every day.

"I think the hardest transition to business for me was getting into the mode of doing as much in my business on a daily basis as I did in basketball, but the daily work is what was required to be good, to be successful.

"With athletics, I had the thrill of the game to keep me going. I didn't really have that initially in business. In order to stay motivated, I had to actually put notes and pictures on my mirror at home, in my closet, on my refrigerator, on my car dashboard, and on my desk at work. The images gave me the mental stimulation of what I was trying to accomplish.

"In basketball, I had to pick up the ball and shoot every day. I had to do the same thing with the business. I had to remember to make some phone calls every day, executing something. Also, having the motivational notes and having pictures reminded me I needed to do something today, this day, and every day."

(Magee) "When we learned about multi-level marketing, it was sort of our only option if we wanted a better life. We were happy and blessed with three wonderful children, but after I left my job to stay home with the children, we were starting to go into debt, juggling our money on what to pay. We certainly weren't living high on the hog at all—just the basics. We were happy, but we really, really were dead broke, just dead broke. We had no savings at all. When this idea came along to have a business of working with other people to build a lot of little businesses, it seemed like a good thing to do."

Defining Roles

(Magee) "I think when the business was laid out, nobody said 'This is what the men do, and this is what the women do.' Everything sort of fell into place like that, though. Having Jack as the upfront person who was out talking to people about networking, marketing, and having home meetings with them seemed natural. That worked out well for us because then I could be home in the evenings with the children most of the time. I took care of all the behind-the-scenes details—all the product ordering, all the paperwork, etc.

"The business has gotten a lot more sophisticated. When we started, we didn't use computers for ordering. We had to write out all of the orders and call them in by phone. Often, I would check over all the paperwork from business owners in our group to be sure everything was correct. You could easily lose forty, fifty, or sixty dollars a week if somebody didn't add up things properly. Then we had to get the money to the bank, praying nothing would bounce. The paperwork could get mind-boggling, but it had to get done. Jack and I wanted a change in our lives badly enough to do the necessary work, and we did what had to be done."

Employee to Business Owner

(Jack) "Drive or ambition for our own business was important and necessary if we were going to succeed. We needed the drive because we didn't have a boss giving us a plan or telling us what needed to be done.

> "DRIVE OR AMBITION FOR OUR OWN BUSINESS WAS IMPORTANT AND NECESSARY IF WE WERE GOING TO SUCCEED."

"I went through a series of things in my own mind. As I said, never having been in business for myself and having to learn about interpersonal conversation with people took time. Magee and I read lots of books and applied what we learned. We talked to people about family, their jobs, and things they liked to do, and sitting down with new people face-to-face got easier over time."

Gas Stations to the Conference

(Magee) "We had been getting together with our teams pretty much every week, and then we were told about a big meeting held at one of the hotels in DC. People were coming not only from this area, but from many other states, as well. The tickets cost seventy dollars for the two of us to attend, not including the hotel. We didn't even consider staying overnight as we just couldn't afford it.

"Seventy dollars out of a budget without an extra dime seemed impossible. I remember saying to Jack, 'Well, we just don't have the money. We can't go,' and he just smiled at me and replied, 'Well, we have products we can sell.'

"I decided the best thing to do would be to sell the concrete floor cleaner and our liquid all-purpose cleaner to gas stations. I loaded our three children in the car and drove from gas station to gas station. I drove up, found the owner or some of the employees, and I would ask, 'May I talk to you a minute about a great product that takes grease off your hands?' I would then start my demo, putting black shoe polish on my hands, and then poured the cleaner over my hands. I'd wipe it off with a towel and show them how well the cleaner worked. Many of the people I talked to bought from me. I think they just felt sorry for me—this lady driving up in a beat-up old car and three kids in the back seat. As I said earlier, we learned to do what had to be done, and going to the conference was very important at the time.

"I don't think I earned the whole seventy dollars in profit, but I got us close enough so we could add an extra fifteen or twenty dollars and get to the conference. I'm sure we didn't go to all of it, but we went to enough of it to make it a real business for us. We saw hundreds of other people at the conference, which added to our excitement and belief."

(Jack) "Well, not many people will say no to Magee. She is always happy, excited, and her personality attracts people to her. Whether you are naturally outgoing or quiet, I learned to teach our team the importance of interacting and talking with others. Although challenging sometimes, I am not intimidated by approaching people now, as I was when we were getting started. Reaching out to other people about a business opportunity can certainly feel a little uncomfortable, especially when we know the person we're approaching might feel somewhat uneasy about it. We had to realize suggesting a business and offering to work with a person was not something most people often experienced. Then I had to learn how to have meaningful conversations with people; if I was going to work with these people, I had to get to know them.

"I also had to learn how to call people on the phone and make appointments, which I developed through practice. My biggest fear was being questioned about what I was doing and whether I could handle the questions. Could I lead these people forward? I knew I would have to teach them to be able to handle the questions, too.

"I have found success is a growth process. I had to figure out what I needed to know, and then I had to decide how to acquire that knowledge—the how to, so to speak—no matter what endeavor. It didn't take long for me to make the connection between coaching and mentorship. The more I learned and began to understand mentoring, the more enthusiasm I got about Magee and I having a large team and having a better life. We got to the point where our own enthusiasm and mentoring began to work together to give us the vision we're going to make it. It helped to keep us going.

"At each place in my life, I had mentors. In this business, my mentor was my sponsor, who's been extremely successful. Before then, I was mentored by my coaches in high school and college, and of course, my parents. One of the greatest things I learned was the fact repetition can give you success. When we do the right things over and over, we can make good changes for ourselves and others. The more we do something—the more repetitions—the better we become at it."

No Interruptions

(Magee) "Our hard work paid off, and we could see our team growing tremendously and our product sales became consistent. We faced many challenges, and one very unexpected challenge came along years later when I was diagnosed with breast cancer. I know disease and illness are different for each person, but as for me, I never had a moment when I took breast cancer as a death sentence.

> "OUR HARD WORK PAID OFF, AND WE COULD SEE OUR TEAM GROWING TREMENDOUSLY AND OUR PRODUCT SALES BECAME CONSISTENT."

"I really credit a lot of my positive attitude about the diagnosis to my upbringing. Both my mother and father were extremely optimistic people, and they instilled that attitude in me. Also, Jack has always been my rock, and I had total faith in my surgeons. I pretty quickly made the hard decisions, and honestly, I just felt so blessed I never believed cancer was going to be anything but a tempo-rary annoyance. I believed I would heal and get better. In the meantime, I couldn't just roll over and forget about life. I had a family. Although the boys were older and on their own, I saw I had a lot of life ahead of me with my sons, their wives, and children. I didn't want to lie around and feel sorry for myself. I had a business to run. I decided from the beginning I would not become an absent business owner and team leader. I scheduled my treatments and surgeries around my family and business schedule as much as I could. I wore wigs, scarves, and remained active at home and in our business.

"Compared to what some people go through in their lives, this was nothing. I mean some people have such devastating issues in their lives that go on and on. I was healthy, strong, had friends, and I had faith in my God everything was going to be all right.

"Jack tells this story about being very upset the night after we got the diagnosis. He says he was lying in bed thinking about me and maybe wor-rying a little. He said he looked over, and I was sound asleep, apparently not at all concerned. He decided at that point he wasn't going to lie awake and worry about the cancer, either.

"I always had real peace in my heart about it and that everything was going to be fine. Our faith certainly helped us through my illness, other health challenges, and this business. Our faith kept us going."

(Jack) "Magee and I live our lives on faith for the big things, like the breast cancer and other health challenges, and for the situations we face on a daily basis. I personally feel because we are faithful people, we needed to keep achieving for ourselves and to help others. We wanted our actions and success to help others believe. I was taught to put work behind my faith, so I had to develop a passion for what I wanted to do. When we started, we needed the money badly. I knew I had to get out and do the necessary work."

Sharing Success

(Jack) "In our business, once you reach a certain level—which we have achieved—you earn not only monthly bonuses, but large annual cash awards and glamorous all-expense-paid trips. Many people have a goal of wanting to go to Hawaii, and Magee and I have been more than twenty times—free! We're very proud to have others on our team who've done the work, grown their business, and now they get the rewards and trips, too.

"Seeing someone else succeed because of your efforts is very fulfilling. The money's nice, but helping another person succeed is most gratifying. I just wish more people would do it.

"Magee and I have a great life. We keep at it hoping more people will decide what they want, put aside distractions, find themselves a mentor who will help them focus, and work through the repetitions that can lead them to success.

"In our business, we have relationships that never have to end. We love those relationships, and we enjoy getting together and helping each other with some of the trials of business ownership. We get to help people for the rest of our lives."

Words of Wisdom from Jack and Magee Spencer

Planning . . . (Jack) "As new business owners, we had to start from zero and plan out everything from that point to wherever we wanted to eventually go. Make things happen on a daily basis. Set goals and plan for the next day. Be sure to also look way out into the future, several years out, so you can gauge what is required now to get where you want to be later."

Balance . . . (Magee) "People talk so much about getting balance in their lives. I definitely wanted to do whatever I needed to be successful in our business; however, my priority was still to be a great mother. I did not want to get down the road, look back, and feel like I did not spend enough time with my children or had ignored them or had not done enough.

"I really had to work it out myself, and I came up with two things most parents can do. Very simply, when I was with the boys, I wouldn't answer the phone. I never would say, 'Sorry, boys, I've got to get the phone.' I did not want to make them feel like the person on the phone was more important than they were. Consequently, when I was playing with them, reading to them, or feeding them, I was 100 percent with them.

"Another thing I did was to really learn to manage my time well. When the children were napping, I would do things then. I was pretty strict about a reasonable bedtime. I had all the boys in bed by eight o'clock. I would use my evenings to make the phone calls and do the paperwork, so the kids never were aware. The key to these two tasks—giving my undivided attention and working while my children rested—though simple, the tough part was the consistency. You will find consistency makes the difference in most endeavors."

Marriage . . . (Jack) "I was looking for a loving person. I saw Magee's reaction to children, which was my same reaction. That drew me to her even more so."

(Magee) "I think the best thing about our marriage is we had our eyes open coming in. In other words, look at the total picture when choosing a mate.

"Remember why you married the person in the first place—the qualities you first saw. Treasure them even as the years go by.

"The saying, 'Love must have eyes, but also eyelids,' is true. Things might begin to annoy you or irritate you as the years go by, but learn to shut your eyes to the negative. Figure out how to be best friends and stay best friends. Laugh a lot, and kiss multiple times every day, that's very important."

What Can YOU Do Now?

"You've read our story and our WOWs—Words of Wisdom—now, what about you?"

(Magee) "When considering business, do some homework, but not too much, because you can get too involved in research and talk yourself right out of a good thing. Get some advice from people you respect and admire who are knowledgeable about the type of business, people who have been involved in the business you're interested in. Then go for it!

"Be smart about your financial investment. You don't want to invest more than you can afford to lose."

(Jack) "Some of the basics to master as quickly as possible are planning, work ethic, repetition, and mentorship.

"I think the hardest part of business ownership is mental focus, but setting goals can help you stay focused on the day. At the end of the day, have a little sit down, and chat about what you accomplished in your business. Did you have a plan? How well was it executed? Review what was done, then plan, execute, and review.

"You can learn or improve work ethic if an outcome is important enough to you. The biggest thing is being willing to do what you need to do when it needs to be done, not necessarily when you feel like doing it.

"Learn to seek knowledge and to believe in yourself. Learn repetition—when you're doing the right thing correctly, those repetitive behaviors can give you success.

"Find yourself a mentor—someone who can take you further than you can take yourself. You want someone who has a sincere interest in you and your success."

Dear Reader,

Here is space for your notes, thoughts, or next steps:

THE ACTOR
BLAIR UNDERWOOD

Blair Underwood is an author, entrepreneur, and award-winning actor, producer, and director. He's been successful in television, Hollywood films, and on the stage. In the summer of 2012, Blair headlined the Broadway revival of Tennessee Williams' "A Streetcar Named Desire" – a role that earned him a Drama League Distinguished Performance Award nomination. He has received six NAACP Image Awards.

Blair has appeared on stage, in films, on television shows, and interviews hundreds of times. He remains active in his chosen field as dramatic actor and also pursues other entrepreneurial interests.

HOW DID HE DO THAT?

Taking big steps and filling large shoes has never stopped Blair Underwood in his quest and love of acting and entertaining. Reared with a strong work ethic and a culture of "You can," Blair made the right moves and did the hard work, creating his success as an actor, author, businessman, and philanthropist.

Blair believes different factors drive people. For him, it was a strong desire to succeed, and he didn't like being told "no." If someone told him he couldn't do something, he'd find a way to make it happen. Early in his career, many people discouraged Blair from pursuing acting, but he has proven them wrong.

"When I knew I wanted to become an actor, I cannot tell you how many people said to me—well-meaning people, people who had been down the path of show business—'The road is difficult, and very few people make it in this business. On top of that, you're black, so you should probably not ex- pect great things or realize it might not happen for you.' To me, this was a big 'no.' They were saying 'no' to my passion and my dreams. I was, therefore, driven to prove everybody wrong. Here's more of my story about how I did that . . . "

The Actor's Story

All About Mindset

"I can't tell you how many times I heard the statistic—and those statistics have not changed—how only three percent in the union of SAG [Screen Actors Guild] make a living in this business. I always think of the old adage of the glass half full or half empty. Instead of even thinking it is 97 percent empty, I said, 'OK, if three percent make it, then I'll be one of those three percent!'

"All I have ever asked for, hoped for, and strived for from other people is to have an equal opportunity to succeed. I believe success starts with our mind and how we perceive the road ahead.

"If we perceive the road or life ahead as a static situation, it will not change. We can easily say, 'Well, I'm a male, so I can't do this; I'm black, so I can't do it; or, I'm a female, too short . . . so I can't do this.'

"We can always find a reason if we look hard enough. We don't have to look hard to find those excuses, but if we really think a way out or a way forward is possible—even if we can't see it, which most times we don't—we'll gain faith. We have to believe in what we cannot see. My faith has played a huge part in my life, not just professionally, but personally also, because of what often is not seen, but is prayed for, hoped for, and visualized, before it is realized."

"I HAD TO LEARN WHEN TO PRESS THE RELEASE VALVE, LEAVING ROOM OPEN TO BE SPONTANEOUS AND FREE IN THE MOMENT. WHAT A JUGGLING ACT! I FOUND, IN GENERAL, IF I'M PREPARED, THEN I'VE EARNED THE RIGHT TO BE FREE AND THROW ALL CAUTION TO THE WIND."

Planning Work and Working the Plan

"As an actor, I work extremely hard to make something as realistic and as natural as humanly possible. The reality, though, is acting produces a very unnatural environment, whether I am on stage in front of hundreds of people, or I am on a sound stage with cameras, crew, and everything else. Everything is very unnatural, and I have found I have to plan as much as I can in terms of the preparation of the work.

"I had to learn when to press the release valve, leaving room open to be spontaneous and free in the moment. What a juggling act! I found, in general, if I'm prepared, then I've earned the right to be free and throw all caution to the wind."

Yes, I Know I Can

"In my family, we grew up with positive thinking books—*As A Man Thinketh, I Dare You, Hung by the Tongue, How to Win Friends and Influence People*—all great books. They have a subtle nuance, but a huge, profound difference exists between thinking positively and believing positively. I don't just think positively; sometimes, I know a certain thing will happen, and I'm not stopping until it happens. I can have a hope and a wish, which is positive thinking. For me, once I visualize it, I get certainty, and I am much more driven to make it happen. That's belief.

"We can't wait for something to come our way. We must create those opportunities.

"A buddy of mine recently said, 'Don't follow your dreams.' I love this part, 'Stalk that sucker down until you get it!' I call that a much more proactive concept of following your dreams.

"Working in the entertainment field is a culmination of a number of things. It starts with a belief and how you see it, but it's much more. I will say success does take a support system, and I have been fortunate since childhood through today. I know not everyone has advocates, but steps to success start with your mind, spirit, heart, and soul together, saying, 'I can do this!'

"I happen to be a Christian, but I often say, 'Whatever you believe in, I think it behooves any of us to at least be humble enough to recognize there is something greater than the sum of all its parts—that something is greater than *all* of us.' If you believe in something greater, and it's good, your faith will keep you on the right path, where it all starts. I believe if we pray for a support system, put it out there, pray about it, and believe, it *will* come. We just need to hold onto our belief, and the right things we want will happen."

Discipline is Critical

"Discipline is a critical ingredient in any successful career. Discipline is imperative.

"I remember somebody saying years ago about Madonna, 'It's blonde ambition, and she's maybe not very smart.' I thought quite the contrary. I think someone like Madonna—or anybody with her type of off the chart success—is very wise and extremely disciplined. By the grace of God, this is my twenty-seventh year in the business. I've seen many people come and go. Most of my success is not because I'm talented, but because I am so persistent and won't accept 'no.' In many ways, the talent is, unfortunately, the least important ingredient in a long-standing career. If every person who was talented had a great career, we would see many more people hugely successful in any business, especially in show business. Many other variables come into play.

> "MOST OF MY SUCCESS IS NOT BECAUSE I'M TALENTED, BUT BECAUSE I AM SO PERSISTENT AND WON'T ACCEPT 'NO.'"

"What I have found is those who have longevity do indeed have a strong work ethic, which can be as simple as showing up for work on time. I've seen people lose jobs just for being late. I've seen people lose jobs for not knowing how to treat other people on a set. I've seen people lose jobs because of sexual harassment, speaking out of turn, and crossing the line. All of this relates to discipline, whether it's personal discipline or professional discipline. These bad choices can come bite you in the behind and kill a career. Success isn't about kissing butt—I've never believed in that. Rather, success is about respecting ourselves and giving ourselves the right discipline, the respect, and regard to walk through life with determination and integrity. I think young people operate from a youthful state of mind where they don't want to conform. I did the same thing; I didn't want to conform. I know now I must conform to certain requirements, like starting a shoot at a certain time and knowing my lines—those simple things. To me, this all comes under the canopy of discipline."

Parental Influence

"First and foremost, my parents are my mentors because of the example they live in their personal lives and the way they raised us as a family. Chief among all those tenets was, 'You can do anything.' I will say, too, as an African-American family, one of the things they instilled in us was, 'Don't you ever let your race be a hindrance to you, and don't you ever allow anybody to convince you your race is a hindrance to you, regardless of the history, historical times, or the tradition, or where you are. Our race is a blessing, and it's a gift. Take everything wonderful, powerful, and extraordinary about our race, culture, and history and combine all of those strengths to thrust into the future. Move forward with that.' I think the sense of confidence and pride in who we are is one of the greatest things my parents gave to my siblings and me. They also gave us our faith. They were not being didactic about it and preaching those words, but the way they lived their lives was a wonderful example."

The Impact of Travel

"Being an army brat, we moved in and out of various communities, cities, and states. We had an opportunity to see how people in different communities interacted with each other. I'm talking specifically about race relations, and I always watched my parents and the entire family navigate in and out of all cultures.

"The common denominator of all social situations is the human dynamic, without negating race at all, in fact, just the opposite. It's about never forgetting who you are and about being proud of yourself. Find what bond connects you instead of focusing on the discrepancy. In fact, embrace and celebrate the differences! I've often felt that way in the acting world.

People talk about color-blind casting. My feeling is I don't want you to be blind to my color. I want you to see my color, but I want you to get past your hang-up about my color."

Help in New York City

"When I think about mentors or supporters, I have to mention Ms. Elsie Rudder, who was an elderly Barbadian lady. I lived in her apartment in Brooklyn my first six months in New York. She was a domestic for a family on Park Avenue. Before she would get on the train every morning, she would cook me dinner and leave it in a pot for me. I'd go out for auditions in the freezing, New York cold and come back to my dinner. I would just turn the heat on under the pot of food she left for me, and warm it up. I consider her one of my angels."

High School Teacher

"Marie Maniego was my English teacher, and I did a number of plays with her and her company, Playmaker Fellows, when I was in high school. In my senior year, I was president of the student government club at Petersburg High School, and Ms. Maniego was my mentor. We wanted to get some things done within the school system. She was my sounding board on how to make things happen. I'm most proud of our legacy that year of bringing the Junior ROTC program into Petersburg High School. My dad had led the charge. He tried once before, and then when I became president of student government, we worked together. The ROTC program still exists at Petersburg High School, and I'm most proud of this accomplishment. Ms. Maniego assisted in making it a reality."

Family, Friends, and Faith

"Nobody who's made far reaching life and career goals and achieved them has done it on his or her own, including me. I think if we believe the misnomer that we can make it on our own, it's the beginning of the end. People in our circle, faith in a greater power, and our belief all come together to aid us. We must know a certain goal or dream can happen for us, especially when we feel like it is our calling. But we must also be humble enough to know and say, 'You know what, God, I want to do Your will at the end of the day.' If what I want is not the will of my God, then it's not to be. Unfortunately, we sometimes don't know His will until we've walked the path, and we have to follow what we feel our heart is telling us.

"I don't even know how I would live my life without a strong faith. The world has too many pitfalls, distractions, haters, and negative dynamics to think I'm going to walk this walk and not get scathed if I try to do it all by myself. I do know God protects us all from evil seen and unseen. I am grateful I haven't seen a whole lot of the evil, not because it doesn't exist, but because those obstacles have been removed."

The Business of Acting

"The business of acting is an entirely different beast, which can beat you down with the opportunities, or lack thereof, and the cut-throat nature of show business. It is what it is.

"I often describe myself as happily discontent. I appreciate and am humbled for the opportunities I've been given, first by God and those instruments, those people, who have come along the way to open doors. In this stage of my life, I'm not concerned about walking through the opened doors, but I care more about opening doors for others to attain their dreams, whatever they may be.

"I've discovered my purpose in a broad sense, and it is finding a way to allow other people to find their purpose. Sometimes, it's just inspiring other people so they know, 'Yes, you can do it!'

"Of course, everybody's path is different. My path is not somebody else's path. It's going to be unique for every person and their unique script to follow.

"This is all easy to say in retrospect, but show biz is a hard road, one I wouldn't want anybody to try to walk alone."

WOW

Words of Wisdom from Blair Underwood

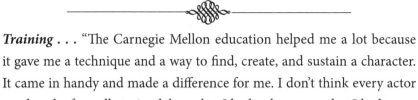

Training . . . "The Carnegie Mellon education helped me a lot because it gave me a technique and a way to find, create, and sustain a character. It came in handy and made a difference for me. I don't think every actor needs to be formally trained, but what I had to learn, or what I had to re-learn, was how to have fun. I had to remember why I love entertaining in the first place, and it is to do just that—to entertain an audience.

"We can get so bogged down in the headiness of the work and the craftsmanship, but at the end of the day, our job is to entertain an audience, communicate a message, and tell a story. In terms of acting and theater, the best teacher is real life, just being an observer of the world around you."

Technology . . . "The beauty of today's sophisticated and super speed technology is how it has empowered you. It has empowered all of us. You can use technology to promote yourself and shine a light on your talent. You can take a camera, or even a phone now, and create a short film. You can tell short stories. You can become a filmmaker with very little money.

"You can do more on your own now, and I would just encourage you to know your power and not wait for a studio executive, network executive, or agent to dub you and dictate your self-worth. You have it before you walk in their door! You even have it before you leave your door.

"One of the most challenging things in an acting career is getting people to see your work in order to hire you so you can promote yourself. You can do your work in your own home, film it, and use it as a tool to help find representation. If you can't find representation, you can use technology as a tool to put yourself online to promote yourself.

"We as artists—in any realm—have been empowered today by the technology at our fingertips. Whether you're an actor, producer, or director, your job in entertainment is to tell a story. In terms of being creative, today's technology can be a benefit."

What Can **YOU** Do Now?

"You've read my story and my WOWs—Words of Wisdom—now, what about you?

"Let me comment on two broad subjects: the work of acting, and being ready.

"I used to say, 'Get as much training in the theatre as possible.' It still holds true, but the caveat is if you are serious about being a performing artist, then get as much time in the theatre and on stage as possible. For anyone who is serious about acting, the creation of characters, telling stories, and affecting an audience by making them laugh, cry, feel, and think, I say, 'That's the beauty of being an actor.' Act and do it as much as possible! You must also learn how to write your ideas down, whether you're a professional, or just an average casual writer. Write them down or type them up, but put your ideas on paper.

"However, if your goal is to be a star, I don't know what to tell you. A lot of people want to be famous. They don't want to act. They want to be renowned, especially in this culture of five or fifteen minutes of fame. Nowadays, people can put themselves on video and be an overnight sensation. In this case, no talent is necessary anymore to become a celebrity. But I can't help with that. I don't know about chasing fame.

"Next, in terms of being ready, you have to make time for the work. Preparation often comprises doing research with a lot of repetition—especially in learning lines. I usually take chunks at a time, whether a page or a paragraph, and do it over and over. By the same token, success comes from drilling lines as much as you can so it's second nature when you release it on stage. Allow yourself plenty of lead time. Take time to repeat your lines. I draft my wife, and now the kids are old enough, to run lines with me. That always helps. Be prepared.

"To see how I might be preparing for a role or other activities in my career, follow me on Facebook at https://www.facebook.com/BlairUnderwood or on Twitter at https://twitter.com/BlairUnderwood."

Dear Reader,

Here is space for your notes, thoughts, or next steps:

THE POLITICIAN
LAWRENCE DOUGLAS WILDER

L. Douglas Wilder became the nation's first elected African-American governor in 1989. The grandson of slaves, Wilder attended segregated elementary and high schools, and went on to college at Virginia Union University. His election as governor was not Wilder's first successful campaign. In 1969, he was elected to the Virginia Senate and later elected and served as lieutenant governor in Virginia, just prior to his gubernatorial race.

HOW DID HE DO THAT?

Governor Wilder credits his mother, Beulah Wilder, for instilling in him an "anything is possible" attitude. If he reached for a goal, he believed he could make it. Mrs. Wilder pushed her children academically, advocated philosophic ideals, and required recitation of poetry. Doug Wilder said his mother made him believe anything was possible, anything was achievable. Governor Wilder used this mindset with every endeavor and believed it gave him an advantage.

"*I am Doug Wilder, an army veteran who served in the Korean War. Thankfully, I made it back home to the US, graduated college, worked in the medical examiner's office, and later studied law and opened a private law firm. I have held four elected offices: mayor, state senator, lieutenant governor, and governor. I lecture at universities, am sought for public policy collaboration, and national broadcast interviews. Here is more about how I did that . . .*"

The Politician's Story

Listening and Speaking

"In public office, we must consider our motivation, and what drives me is people. I listen to people wherever I go, whether at Lowe's, Kroger's, or Food Lion. People feel they can talk with me, something politicians can't buy, because people just don't talk to everybody.

"I know no one can do everything, but I am going to see what I can do for you. I remained steadfast, positive, and I never allowed negativism to stop me. The best way to get me do something is to tell me I can't do it! Oh,

God, I've experienced it: 'You shouldn't put your office in Churchill [historic neighborhood in Richmond, Virginia]. You shouldn't run for office. You shouldn't do this, that, and the other.'

"My mother told me to be as smart as you can, read as much as you can, and learn as much as you can. I never saw anything anyone else did that I couldn't do if I chose to do it, if I chose to take the time to do it. I worked at it. My mother was in agreement with Socrates: 'Know thy right and then proceed.' In other words, make up your mind about what's right, and then you do it. Don't let anybody change you from that. She also believed in public exposure. She had an aunt who would put on these silver teas and would get all of us kids to sing, recite poetry, play the piano, be in a play, or something.

"My mother was a very smart woman. She was a native of Charles City [Virginia], but she was raised in New Jersey. She attended public schools and high school in New Jersey, and came to Virginia when her mother died. She lived with her aunt, and then shortly thereafter, married my father. Since she had been to school in New Jersey—the only person of color in her school and in her class—she was well exposed to being around and competing with whites. She knew she had nothing to be afraid of. Her attitude was a big influence for me, a different perspective from my father, whose parents were slaves. His views were divergent, not submissive at all, but less outspoken. My mother pushed us to speak out no matter what anyone else thought about what we had to say. Her push and drive were instilled in me and my siblings."

Pivotal Points

"I have always said Brown vs. Board of Education changed me around. I saw how nine white men decided, after fifty-six years, America was wrong with Plessy vs. Ferguson. Primarily, black lawyers from Howard University got that case overturned. I knew the system could work, and it could work for people. I said to myself, 'I am in the wrong field here. I need to get out of science studies and get into a system where things happen, and I can be a part of it.'

"I had been to Korea, came back, and had pretty much given up on the nation doing anything to recognize me. I couldn't understand why I would be sent to fight in Korea for other people's rights, and I didn't have any here in the US. I think the whole thrust was I couldn't go to law school here in Virginia. Back then, the state of Virginia would pay the tuition to prevent blacks from attending college here. Howard was the only school I applied to. Luckily, I got a couple lawyers I knew to write references for me—Roland D. Ealey and Colston Lewis—and fortunately, I was accepted. I was on the GI Bill, and I had saved up a little money.

"When I went up to DC to Howard University, I almost flunked out. I was so happy to have a chance to spend, I bought a car with my savings and did everything else except study. Washington, DC was just paradise for me! I went to all these clubs, and I was waiting tables out at the Bolling Air Force Base Officers' Club. I had a ball, but was failing several courses. One day, I was walking up Georgia Avenue to take a final examination and saw some men down in a hole. A water main had broken in the street, and these men were in a muddy mess digging a ditch. I never will forget it. I said, 'That's where I'm going to end up—digging a ditch.' It was an epiphany of what a fool I'd been. I was lucky enough to get back from Korea—so many guys didn't make it—and here I was with a second shot, a real good chance, and I was going to blow it. I said, 'If I get through this year, no more problems from me.' I was able to pretty much finish the first year with a C average, but the second and third year—shoot—it wasn't even close. I had no trouble finishing law school and moved on once I completed that."

> "I HAD BEEN TO KOREA, CAME BACK, AND HAD PRETTY MUCH GIVEN UP ON THE NATION DOING ANYTHING TO RECOGNIZE ME. I COULDN'T UNDERSTAND WHY I WOULD BE SENT TO FIGHT IN KOREA FOR OTHER PEOPLE'S RIGHTS, AND I DIDN'T HAVE ANY HERE IN THE US."

Law was Paramount

"I was never as interested in politics as much as I was interested in the law. I only got involved in politics later, after I didn't see the kind of representation needed for the issues and the causes of people. I later felt I wanted to be a part of the decision-making processes, and my professors instilled it in me. One such professor, Samuel Dewitt Proctor, a former president of Virginia Union, taught me about what he called 'the polity [pol'i-tee], p-o-l-i-t-y, polity.'

"He said, 'You want to be a part of the polity. You want to be a part of what makes things happen, what makes things work. You want to get out there.'

"In other words, someone else shouldn't always make the decision. The important thing is not just about being able to go to an integrated school or an integrated restaurant. The question is who decides. The law is the sum total of *all* of man's experiences, and to the extent the law is, then why should I not be a part of making those laws and interpreting those laws and practicing the law to the extent of representing those people who are called upon to obey the law?"

Don't Stop, Keep Going

"Knowledge is so vast, and we have so much to learn. We can't learn enough. My drive has always been to learn more, and I do every day. I believe government needs to be perfected. After having served as governor, one of the reasons I came back and ran for mayor of Richmond [Virginia] is I saw what I described as a cesspool of inefficiency and ineffectiveness in the city government. We changed the form of government and set forth a strong mayoral form. I didn't want to run for it, but some said, 'Well, right now we don't have anybody else to step in to do it. You're going to have to do it.' I said, 'OK, I will do it for at least one term.' And, I did it, and I did not seek another term because I felt we were at the threshold of where we had set the course and others could step in.

"Now, does that mean I'm finished with being involved with public life? No. It means I'm finished with being involved with elected office. A lot of people make that mistake, particularly young people. I try to disabuse them of it. To be involved in politics doesn't mean you have to be in elected office. Some of the most important positions in this country are held by people who don't have to run for any office—Secretary of State, Secretary of Defense, Supreme Court Justice, Federal Reserve Chairs—just to name a few—they have influence. Our younger people haven't gotten the message. They really don't know what comprises the polity. They don't know.

> "TO BE INVOLVED IN POLITICS DOESN'T MEAN YOU HAVE TO BE IN ELECTED OFFICE. SOME OF THE MOST IMPORTANT POSITIONS IN THIS COUNTRY ARE HELD BY PEOPLE WHO DON'T HAVE TO RUN FOR ANY OFFICE."

"The thing we've got to do is the thing that possibly would not get done if we did not do it. We are missing this link in society today. We need to develop shark's teeth. Sharks have all their teeth at birth. They don't grow them. They might grow longer, but if this set is gone, the other ones are ready to move on up front. We need to do the same. When one leaves a position or office, we ask who's going to take their place? We don't take someone's place—we take our own place. That's what the shark's tooth does. This tooth didn't take the place of this one; this tooth is here. It grows on its own, just like the other ones did.

"We need to develop a mind for agitation in stirring up and demanding what is right, and criticizing what is wrong. We need to develop this in young people. Even if some feel fortunate enough to move through and become a part of what I described as the polity, the door doesn't stay open by itself. I feel fortunate to be here, and I feel I have an obligation to make life better, not only for myself, but for others. I know I still have a purpose, which is another reason why I'm not going into what some would call a general restful retirement. I am doing everything I can to make the world a better place for everybody to the extent I can. I keep going, because once I found my purpose, I didn't stop. This is something maybe we could all do, but how is your purpose defined for you? That is the question."

WOW

Words of Wisdom from Doug Wilder

Accomplishments . . . "Life does not have to be complicated. You don't have to reach for the top. Reach for what it is you can accomplish, and never stop reaching.

"Don't be satisfied with materialism. How many cars, rings, and necklaces can you buy? Can you get along just fine with one?"

Steadfastness . . . "My mother said—and it has stayed with me—'Don't rush to judgment, and you need to know just who you are. When you do those two things, make up your mind. Then once you make up your mind, stay the course. Don't even change your mind if I tell you to, even if I say I disagree with you. If you think you're right and feel you are not doing harm to any others, you stay where you are, and you do that.'"

Education . . . "Everything gets back to education. Dumb people don't run anything, and you've got to be as smart as you possibly can. Don't let anyone tell you education is not important."

Integrity . . . "Keep your word. Don't say you're going to do something unless you're going to do it. You don't have to lie. You've got to keep your word."

What Can  Do Now?

"You've read my story and my WOWs—Words of Wisdom—now, what about you?

"If you want to consider elected office, you must have expertise to represent well, which means being able to make informed decisions. To serve capably in elected office, you need to be able to master the office you are seeking. For example, if you plan to run for a school board seat, you should know something about management, personnel, curriculum, or educational structure. Love of children is not sufficient to serve on a school board, no more than love of people qualifies anyone to seek election to a local or state governing body.

"Also, don't be tempted to seek one office as a stepping stone to another. Seek the position you are really interested in. In elected office, we are signing up to be servants. Let's serve with our constituents in mind, not ourselves.

"If you are planning to seek office, and I'm consistent with this, you need to be able to think before you speak. What I do quite frequently in response to something is write down my thoughts or reaction, then hold onto it for a while. I wait to see if I could express my opinion another way or not, and sometimes I realize the best response is no response at all. You don't have to respond to everything. You don't have to provide grist for their mill."

Dear Reader,

Here is space for your notes, thoughts, or next steps:

A Note to Parents, Guardians, Relatives, and Friends

Several people have asked me—including some of those profiled in this book—whether I heard any common themes as I conducted the interviews. Yes, common themes showed up as lessons I can apply and use to enhance my life.

Please join me in encouraging our children and telling them they can do anything. This is an easy step. Anytime you see a child struggling over a task or hesitant to take on a challenge, say to him, "You can do it." Teach them work ethic by making them work. Chores around the house and helping neighbors are good starts. Remind them to watch their time, reinforce the importance of punctuality and let them know tardiness can lead to lost opportunities.

Education, education, and education is the great equalizer. Almost everyone profiled in *How Did They Do That?* mentioned the importance of a solid educational foundation. Emphasize education, and perhaps continue studies for yourself in some form or another. Support children with their school work and be a part of their school activities. We could all benefit from reading a lot more on a wide mix of topics from varied sources.

Consider allowing young people in your life to play an instrument. The absence of this talent can cause separations from acquaintances they have made or close doors to friendships and experiences. I started piano lessons and didn't stick with it. I regret my decision to this day. People who do know the language of music say it expands their minds when they are approaching other seemingly unrelated tasks.

We shouldn't let children grow up just relying on us. As hard as we try to do right and to do well, at times we will fall short, and sometimes we fail. Share your belief in God with your friends and children around you; let them know God will always be there for them when people are not around to fulfill their needs.

Take time for solitude. By discovering yourself in your quiet times, you can have more thoughtfulness to offer, and you might find personal esteem. Finally, be true to yourself and others. Hug, kiss, and care for your friends and family.

These are my notes. What did you write down?

Deborah Tompkins Johnson

Additional Resources

Herman Boone

Remember the Titans, An American film produced in 2000 by Jerry Bruckheimer and Chad Oman, and directed by Boaz Yakin. Inspired by real events, the plot was conceived from a screenplay written by Gregory Allen Howard. Music: Trevor Rabin, Rating: PG (USA). en.wikipedia.org: http://disneydvd.disney.go.com/remember-the-titans-directors-cut.html

Kate Koob

Guest of the Revolution by Kate Koob
1982, Thomas Nelson, Inc.

Inside a U.S. Embassy: Diplomacy at Work by Shawn Dorman
2011, Potomac Books, Inc.

The American Foreign Service Association
http://www.afsa.org/OutreachPrograms/InsideaUSEmbassy.aspx

Carl McNair

Where Valor Rests—Arlington National Cemetery
www.wherevalorrests.org

Blair Underwood

Carnegie Mellon University
www.cmu.edu

Co-founder, Artists for a New South Africa
www.ansafrica.org

Doug Wilder

L. Douglas Wilder School of Government and Public Affairs (at Virginia Commonwealth University)
http://www.wilder.vcu.edu/

The Wilder Collection at Virginia Union University http://www.vuu.edu/library/archives_special_collections/the_wilder_collection.aspx

Deborah Tompkins Johnson

www.deborahtompkinsjohnson.com

Photography

Herman Boone
Courtesy American Program Bureau, Inc.

Niki Hall
Grace Sun, Photographer

Kathryn Koob
Nicole Priebe, Photographer

Doug Wilder
Courtesy Virginia Commonwealth University, L. Douglas Wilder School of Government and Public Affairs